HOMEWORK

"The city is like a great house, and the house in its turn a small city."

—Leon Battista Alberti

"All buildings really want to be houses."

—Mark McInturff

McInturff Architects

HOMEWORK
New Houses | Changed Houses | Not Houses

Mark McInturff, FAIA
Julia Heine

Contents

6   Variety, Detail, Construction

New Houses

10   Chain Bridge House
20   A House in a Clearing
30   Library House
40   House. Pool. Garden.
50   House on Indian River Bay
58   McDaniel Marsh House
66   Chesapeake Bay House
74   Reid Beach House
80   Singh Hoysted Live/Work
88   Rappahannock Bend Summer House
92   Ridge House
96   House on Tilghman Creek
104   House on Deep Creek Lake
106   Del Ray House
108   Multigenerational House in Jamaica

Changed Houses

112   Live/Work
120   Georgian Modern
126   Woodmont 17th Floor
132   ADU Crestwood
136   Truss House
140   Woodley Park House & Garden
146   Porter Street House
150   House on Maxmore Creek
156   21st Century Cabin
162   Georgetown House
170   Ranleigh Road Library
174   Hutner Porch & Pool
180   López Forastier-Hellmann House
184   Edmund Street House
188   House in Kenwood
192   House on Poplar Avenue
196   43rd Street Townhouse
198   Xia Yang House

Not Houses

202   Greencourt Innovation Center
212   Parker Metal
218   Urban Courtyard Apartments
224   Watergate East Lobbies
232   The Writer's Center
236   Politics and Prose
242   Art Works Now
246   Georgetown Mixed-Use
248   St. Michaels Community Center

250   Firm Profiles
251   Project Credits
254   Selected Published Works

Variety, Detail, Construction

Our firm built its reputation designing houses, and they still form a large part of our practice. This most intimate of building types involves working closely with the most highly involved and engaged clients, finding a unique form that is both a true fit to their program and a real expression of their lives.

The particularity of each client and site results in endless variation within this single building type, in the details and the range of opportunities, with no two the same.

When we begin a new project, we have no idea in what direction things are going to go. We find that out as we go along, taking cues from our clients, the site, the people who will build the project, and local influences. The end is almost always a surprise. In looking at the proofs for this book, it is the variety from project to project that strikes me.

There are reasons for this variety. First, our buildings reflect who we are designing for because all good projects do. In Washington, we have the good fortune to have a diverse population, international, and well-educated. It has been said that the only industry in Washington is ideas, so we deal with talented people who understand that there should be much thought invested into their project. Given the opportunity to interact with interesting people of wildly different backgrounds, we must revel in it.

While all our work is in some way evolved from the origins of the modern movement in architecture, we see no reason to confine ourselves to one of the many branches of the tree that makes up modernism. Not all of our buildings look alike or are even overtly similar. We have no predetermined house style, or style of house. We do not believe in doing that, and we actively believe in not doing it.

Equally, we would not confine our clients or the communities they live in to one way of doing things. We can make buildings of steel and glass, or of stone and wood, or brick, or clapboard, or metal. And we do all those things, and versions and variations of each can be seen in the following pages.

We make buildings that are colorful inside or out or both, and buildings that take their coloring from the nature of the materials from which they are made, with no artificial color applied at all.

We make buildings with built-in contrasts of new and old, and buildings where new and old blend seamlessly.

We can make buildings that stand out from their settings as well as ones that blend in, whether the setting is a bucolic natural site, or an historic urban street.

Going forward, we will continue to design houses as the core of our practice; they continue to offer the greatest creative range, and level of a client's emotional commitment. But some of the houses won't be *houses*.

Although it is often assumed that many architects are specialist—focusing only on residential, or commercial, or institutional—a good architect can be a generalist, and one who designs houses can translate those skills to other types of projects—an office, a hotel, a theater, a community center.

We have been fortunate to be asked to design a variety of building types. But, as we approach one that is new to our practice, we don't change our design process at all. It is still highly interactive, iterative, and very personal.

We design all buildings as if we are designing a house, because we believe all buildings should want to be houses—a project to which the clients are fully committed, that is welcoming, nurturing, protective, stimulating, and serene. Places where people can comfortably be together or be apart. And, of course, all should be reflective of those for whom they are designed.

Our residential work taught us to be good listeners, and we have carried that over to our larger projects, which have involved clients with the same commitment to their projects as our house clients.

This has not only been a matter of luck. We are proud of our working relationships with our clients, many of whom return to us for additional work.

A client for whom we have designed a house may ask us to work on something else with which they are involved—a hotel, a community center, offices, a bookstore café, an arts education nonprofit. The collaborative process developed during the original project is already familiar and easily flows into the development of the new work.

The larger projects have offered new ways to build with an attention to community, which we see as an expanded version of a family. Whether it is the lobby or courtyard of a multifamily building, or a community center or art school, and regardless of the economic demographic of the users, we have been interested more and more in making buildings that involve bringing people together when outside of their own residential setting. This is satisfying both architecturally (as we get to make new kinds of spaces) and socially (as we get to serve a broader clientele), including some who may not normally have access to, or the benefit of, their own architect.

Within all this variety, there are core beliefs that carry through our work, even as new ideas and technologies are introduced, and as we have begun to take on a larger variety of scales and types of projects.

We are particularly interested in how a building or a space is made, in the structure that holds it up, and the way its parts are put together. Not only do we think this adds an eloquence to a space, but it tells the story of its making. Architecture can be about just that—its pieces and how it is constructed.

Columns and beams and walls and foundations are doing a lot of work. We could choose to cover all that behind generic materials, such as drywall, or we can expose the parts we feel contribute to understanding the way the building is made. These elements provide a rhythm, scale, and a level of detail to what might otherwise be mute space. The history of architecture can be read through the evolution of the making of these elements.

McInturff Architects, now in its fourth decade, remains, by intent, a small practice. We are this size in order to maintain design quality, and to allow me to remain more of a designer than manager.

Holding at around a half dozen all in, with minimal turnover, makes us more like a family than a corporate culture. Our long history working together gives us a lot of muscle for a small firm, and a lot of experience as a team. In Peter Noonan and David Mogensen we have decades of experience working together in the studio. Jeff McInturff and Julia Jeffs bring tremendous talent and the digital literacy native to the newer generations of architects.

This is our fourth book with Images Publishing, with the first in 2001, and the others following at seven- or eight-year increments, allowing enough time between volumes to make a completely new body of work. Julia Heine has worked on all four books, doing most of the photography, all the coordination, and the difficult job of editing my ramblings.

Going full circle, I conclude with a quote I love from the introduction Michael J. Crosbie wrote for our first book, *In Detail*:

> "Mark McInturff's choice to keep his practice small and personally manageable has preserved for him those very aspects of architecture that attracts us to it.
>
> For young architecture students looking forward to that day when their dreams will become built reality, and for older architects looking backward from the lofty peaks of principaldom where one's designs can be recognized only in their broadest conceptual outlines, McInturff's architecture reminds all of us that the joy of architecture is in the journey, and in the very parts we can grasp with our hands."

It gives me great pleasure to know that others can perceive the priorities that we have set for ourselves and our work, and hope those goals are still apparent throughout the work that, twenty years later, is presented here.

Mark McInturff, FAIA
Bethesda, Maryland, United States 2022

New Houses

Chain Bridge House

Arlington, Virginia
2018

This house, located in a neighborhood along the Potomac River and close to Washington, DC, is designed for an international couple with complementary backgrounds. One, of Moroccan and European heritage, asked for a courtyard-style house with Moroccan roots. In deference to local weather, a generously proportioned living room, in lieu of the open courtyard, serves as the heart of the house. The other, a retired American businessman, asked for a substantial, sustainable house that was built well and carefully put together, efficient, well detailed, and well organized.

Our response was to create a large, delicate, and transparent inner core of steel, glass, and zinc, flanked with two robust concrete wings clad in stucco, containing the private spaces. All three parts share a common width and structural rhythm. Like a Moroccan house, privacy from the street is achieved through an arrival garden courtyard and a reserved façade, protected by a veil of wood louvers. Then, upon entry—as in the best American houses—the interior, glimpsed through a wall of sliding bronze mesh screens, completely opens through walls of sliding glass doors to a porch, pool, and terraces leading to the wooded ravine below.

The sustainable nature of the house is incorporated into the beauty of the details. Wood louvers provide sun control as well as privacy, as do the recessed motorized shades found throughout the house. Motorized screens pocketed into the porch ceiling can drop down to create a screened porch, and the entire sliding glass wall of the living room can open to it, turning the double-height space into a giant porch. A geothermal heating system with radiant floors, high-efficiency windows, and 14-inch thick insulated concrete exterior walls all contribute to create a house that is luxurious, beautiful, and efficient.

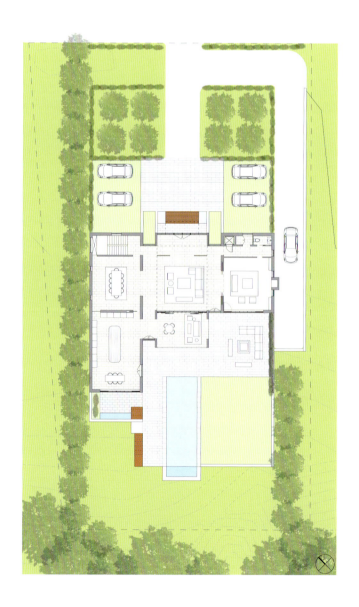

Above Main floor plan
Opposite Entry façade

Left Pool terrace extends the interior living space into the garden
Opposite top Street façade
Opposite bottom Section

Chain Bridge House

Above left View from entry through living room to garden beyond
Above right Double-height living room
Opposite Bridge over entry connects the second-floor bedroom wings

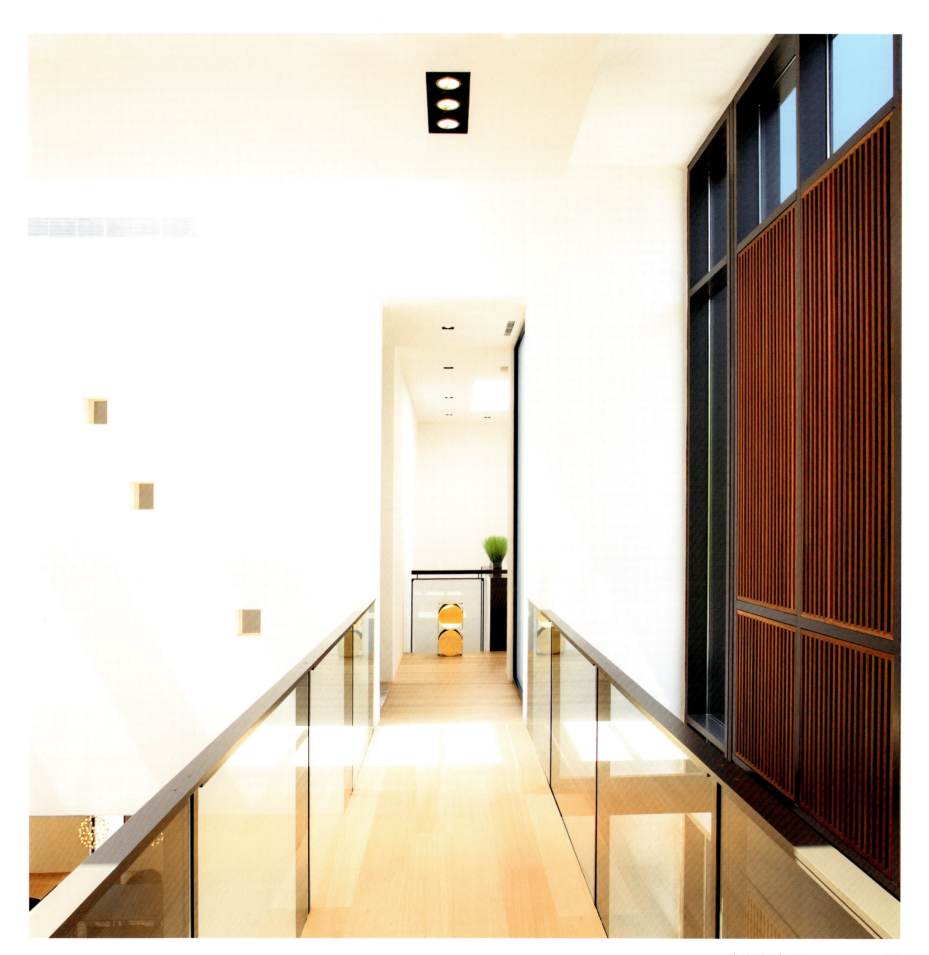

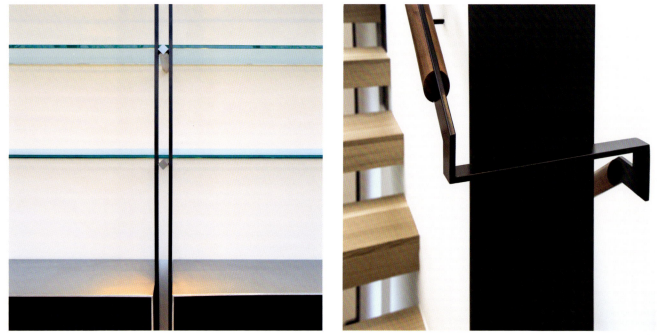

Opposite top Skylights bring natural light into the double-height living room
Opposite bottom left Detail of glass-and-steel bookcases
Opposite bottom right Stair detail
Right Double-height living room with family room beyond

Opposite Views from kitchen island and black granite bar overlook the wooded site
Top Kitchen
Bottom Primary bath

Chain Bridge House

A House in a Clearing

Owings Mill, Maryland
2022

This is a house for a highly particular program and location. On a gently sloping clearing in a forest, it is intended as a filter through which the site flows, unimpeded, while the orientation controls the seasonal sun entering the glassy, transparent house.

Facing the east and west sides of the property, solid masonry walls bookend the body of the house. The long façades facing the slope are entirely glazed, placing the occupants on a platform open above and below to the woods beyond. The south face is pushed toward the tree line, providing full shading from summer sun while admitting the low rays of winter. The north face needs no shading as it opens to the long views into the meadow and trees.

The main spaces—living, dining, kitchen, and workspaces—occupy one end of the platform while a bedroom and gym occupy the other. Separating the two is a masonry core containing bathrooms, stairs, and mechanical spaces as well as two small wood-lined rooms on a minimal second floor.

All materials have been chosen for their authenticity and longevity; steel, wood, concrete, concrete masonry, and glass are the only materials used inside and out. There is no drywall and there is virtually no paint.

Right Site plan
Opposite North façade faces the clearing

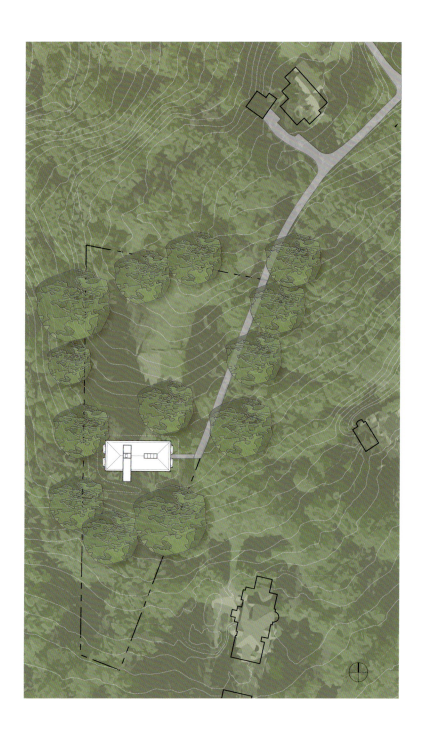

Opposite South façade is shaded by the tall canopy of the woods
Left Entry
Bottom Axonometric diagram

A House in a Clearing 23

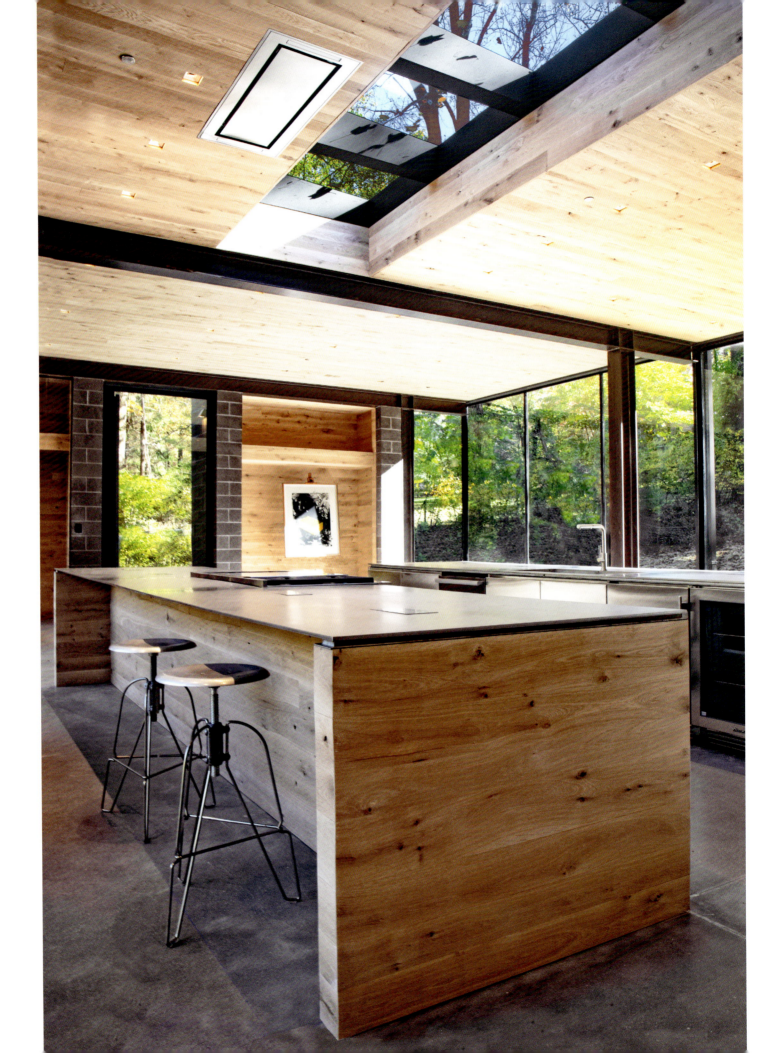

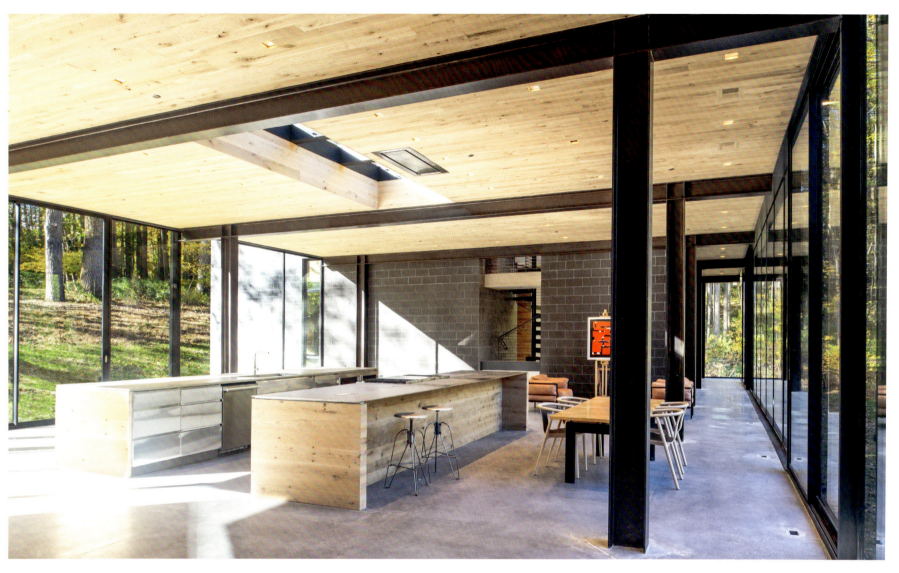

Opposite Kitchen

Above A single large space includes kitchen, dining, living, and work areas

Bottom left Square spiral stair leads to a small second level

Left Kitchen skylight

A House in a Clearing

Opposite Living area
Above Bedroom
Top right Wood-lined second-floor room is adaptable to different functions as needed

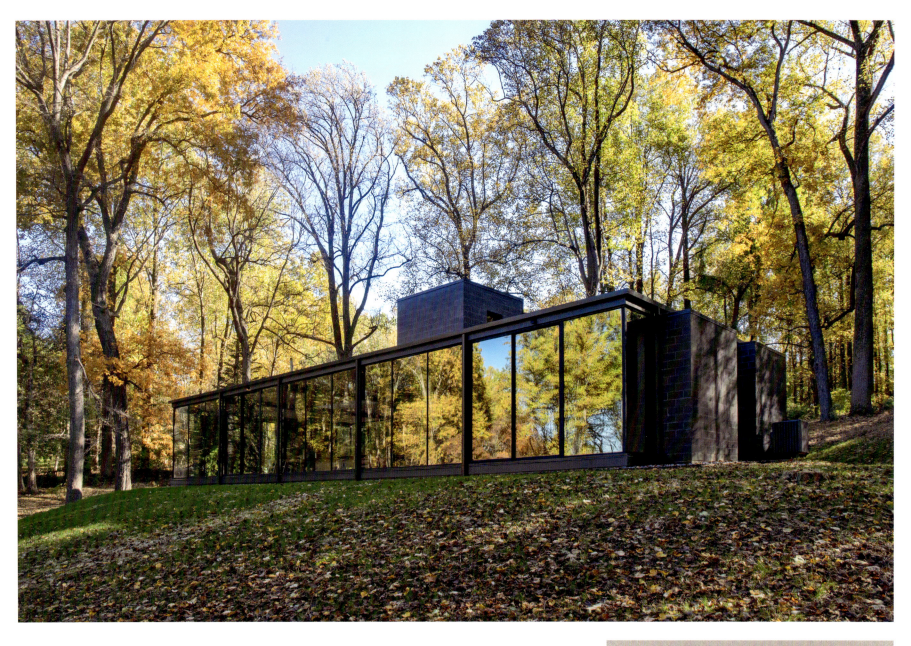

Above Windows on north façade reflect the afternoon sun and surroundings
Right Model
Opposite North façade at dusk

Library House

Potomac, Maryland
2021

This house was designed and intended to be built in two stages, with over a decade between. The first stage included all the typical spaces for family life—living, dining, kitchen, and bedrooms. The second is a library for 10,000 books. This room occupies the center pavilion of the finished three-pavilion house and was left as a clean dark shell in the first build, while the family lived around it in anticipation of, and during the planning for, the second stage.

Now, a carefully detailed and constructed three-level library opens to views over the Potomac River below. The first two levels of the library open and connect directly to the main spaces of the house, completing the original design and providing formal living and dining spaces.

Floating above all this, accessed by a two-story spiral stair, is a glass-floored suspended aerie. Used as a reading space by the owners, the aerie accesses a small outside balcony, floating 30 feet above the ground. Steel windows and mahogany casework extend the existing palette of the house, with lighting and HVAC integrated into and on the shelving.

After over a decade of design and construction, the centerpiece of the project is complete, and the house is finally made whole.

Patience indeed has its virtues.

Top right First-floor site plan
Bottom right Site model
Opposite View of first two levels of library

Opposite Second level of triple-height library with glass reading nook above

Above Lower level of library includes a seating area and large reconfigurable tables for both research and dining

Left View up through glass floor of third-level reading nook

Library House

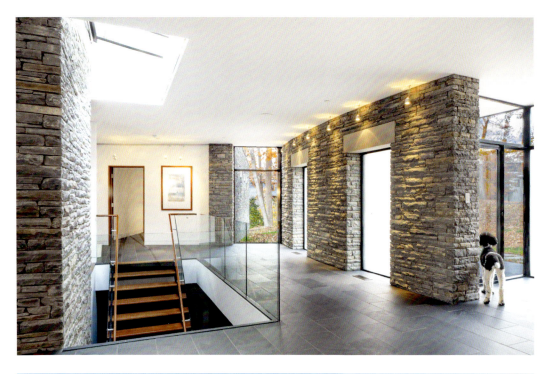

Top Entry
Above Section
Opposite River façade at dusk

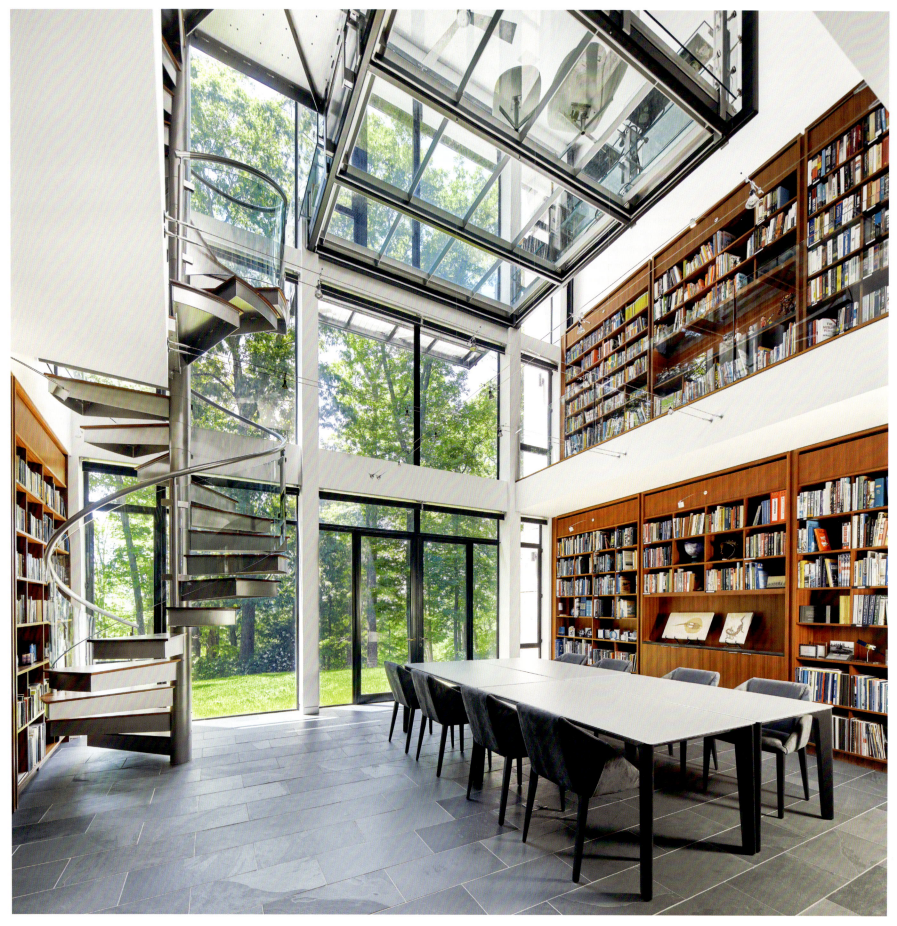

Opposite View up through triple-height space

Right Steel-and-glass spiral stair connects all levels of the library

Left Entry façade
Above Library viewed from entry

Library House

House. Pool. Garden.

Washington, DC
2020

This urban house was designed by its setbacks.

On a corner lot in a leafy urban neighborhood, the long thin shape of this house occupies every legal inch of the site—front, back, and sides. The 75-foot-long swimming pool is allowed outside of the house setbacks. It parallels the length of the house, setting up a house-to-garden relationship not unlike the famed side porch houses found in Charleston.

The house opens up almost entirely to this single side. Inside, pulling the second floor back from the garden façade allows for window walls that extend the full height of the house while terraces and porches connect the house and garden along its entire length. By pulling this long thin house entirely to one side of the site, away from the street, the remaining site is preserved with its topography unchanged and runoff managed. No trees were removed and twenty new ones were planted, creating an open green space where one would expect a house to be. The house takes advantage of natural light from both north (toward the pool) and south (mostly from above) as windows toward the neighbors were deemed undesirable.

This project is a thoughtful and delicate addition to one of Washington's most desirable, highly walkable neighborhoods, in terms of both nature and community. The well-used housing is slowly being renovated to match the standard of the place, so the community is being renewed from within.

Neither the house nor the garden or pool would make sense without the others. As plantings along the street continue to mature, the house will visually claim the entire site between setbacks and street, making a virtue out of a zoning necessity.

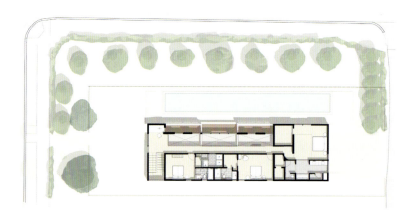

Above First- and second-floor plans
Opposite Entry façade

Opposite Pool façade from street
Right Pool façade at dusk

House. Pool. Garden.

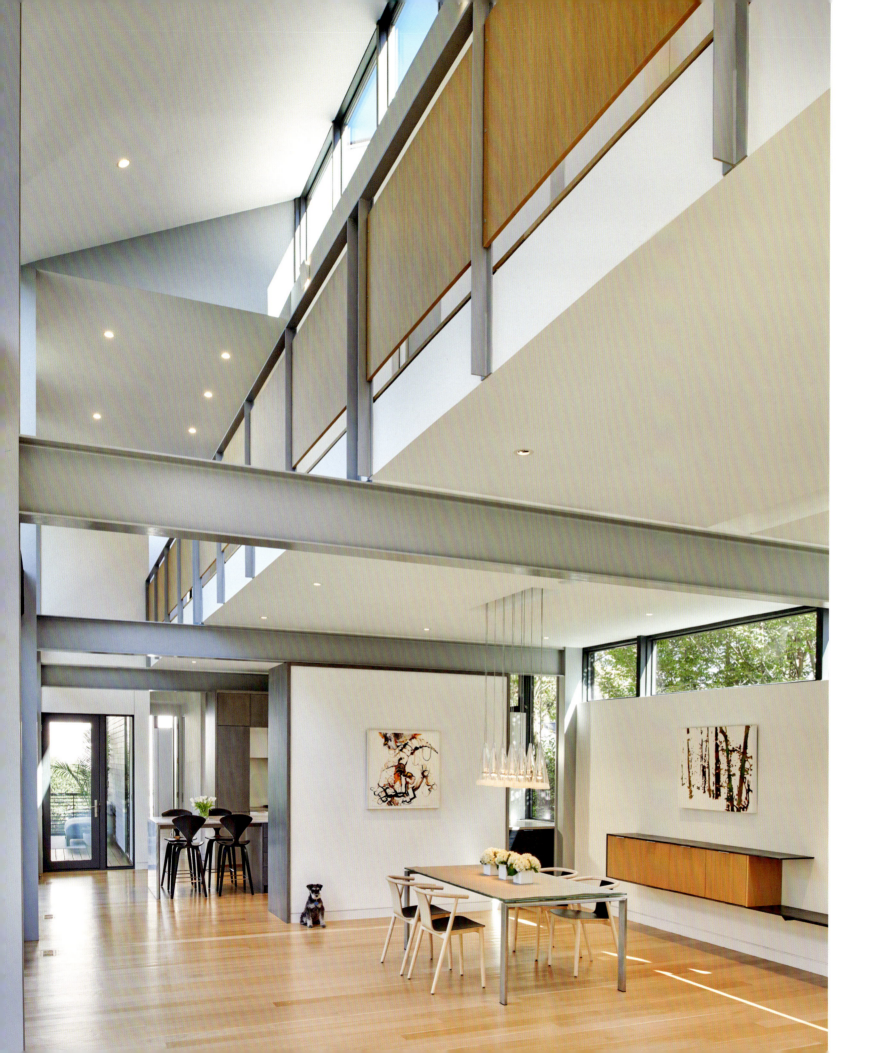

Opposite Dining area with kitchen beyond
Above Living room with stair and entry
Left Model

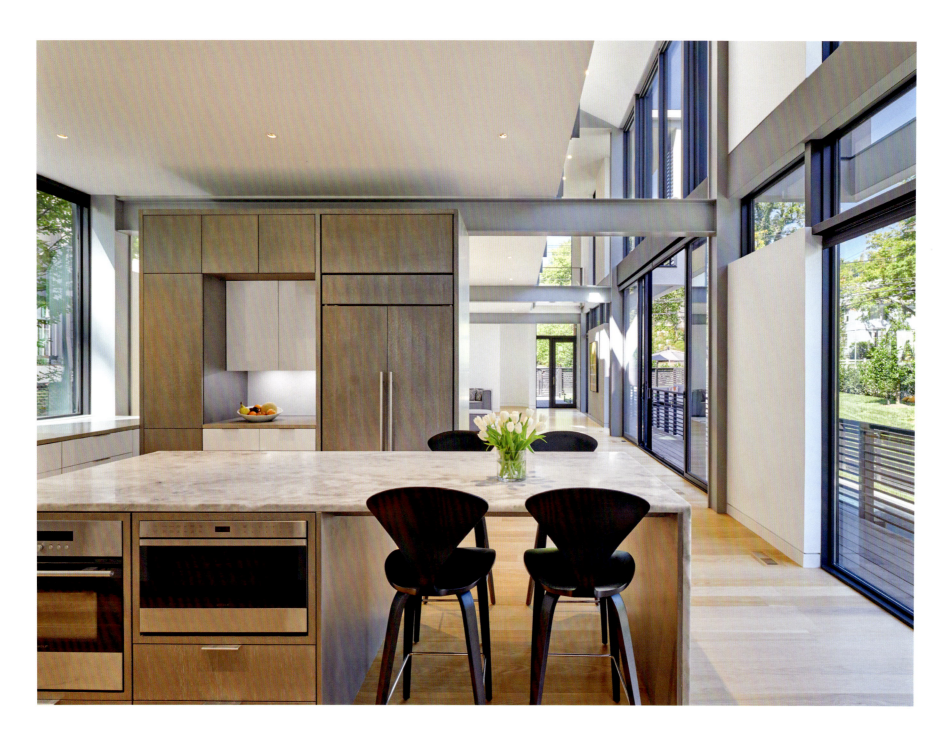

Above Kitchen
Opposite left Bath opens to primary bedroom
Opposite top right Stair handrail detail
Opposite bottom right Double-height gallery

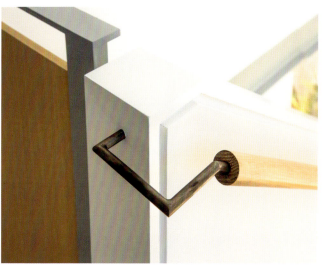

House. Pool. Garden. 47

Opposite Living and dining areas bordered by double-height gallery

Top right Entry façade

Bottom right Sections in series

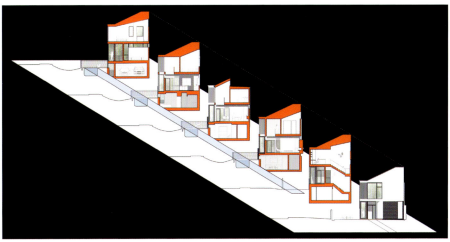

House. Pool. Garden.

House on Indian River Bay

Bethany Beach, Delaware
2019

The Bethany Beach property now occupied by this house became available when a previous house burned to the ground and those owners decided not to rebuild. Our clients lived on an adjacent site and had been planning to renovate their house when this occurred, so, instead, they decided to move next door and start from the ground up.

The site faces west across Indian River Bay, with beautiful views to sunsets across marshes and the water. In plan and massing, two shingled gabled bars bracket an elevated arrival/pool court on the approach side, leading to open living spaces within. The kitchen and bedrooms occupy the gabled volumes; between them, a white modern house is framed and spills out to the site on the bay side.

At every level, outdoor space is maximized, with decks, balconies, hot tub, and stairs opening to the water, culminating in a generous roof deck. Within the living area, with the pool on the east and the bay on the west, it is possible to sit with views to water on both sides.

Right Plans
Opposite Shoreline view

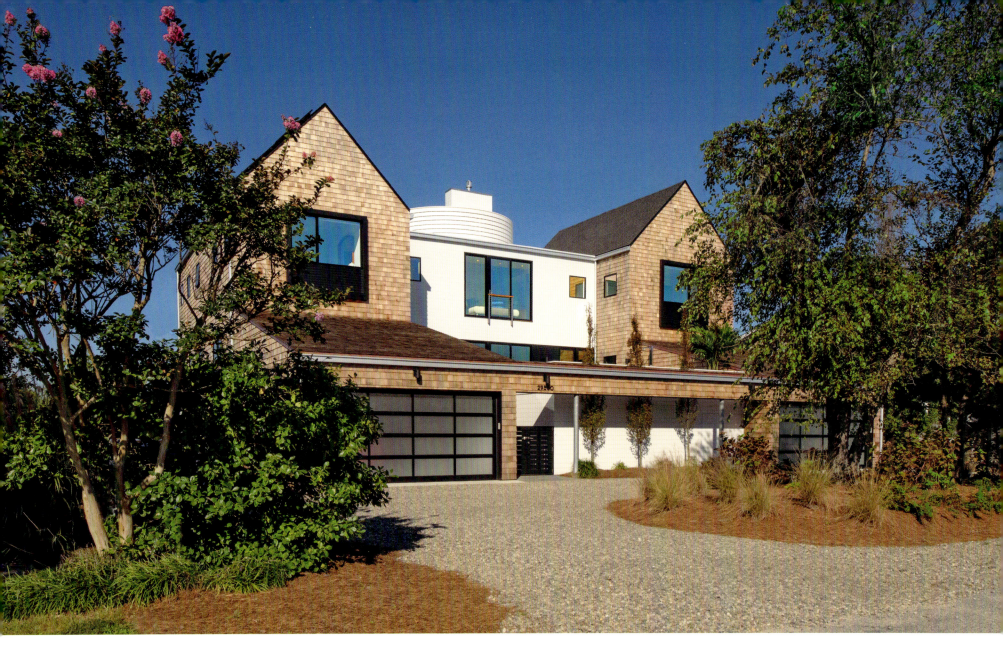

Opposite top Street façade leads to second-level entry court
Opposite bottom left Aerial view
Opposite bottom right Entry court and pool on second level
Left Pool in entry court

House on Indian River Bay

Left Living, dining, and kitchen overlook water views
Top Family room on second-floor mezzanine
Bottom Kitchen

House on Indian River Bay

Opposite Living area with views of Indian River Bay
Above left Second-floor guest room
Above right Main-level rear deck

McDaniel Marsh House

Rehoboth Beach, Delaware
2016

After twenty years of working together on a variety of residential and small commercial projects, this owner/general contractor asked us to design her own house. What followed was a give and take exercise in trust and faith.

Sited on marshy wetlands on the Delaware Bay, the house occupies the only buildable corner of the lot. Directly following the polygonal boundaries of the site in order to maximize the tiny allowed area, the house forms an oblique "L" shape. The interior corner of the L-shape opens out through a tall fan-shaped screened porch. Sliding glass doors on both floors open the rooms directly to this porch, extending the interior to it and to the marsh surroundings.

Douglas fir windows and doors are important to the interior expression, and the use of fir is carried through to interior cabinets and soffits. A dark cork floor recalls the dark water of the marsh, further uniting interior and exterior and serving to ground the simple surfaces of wood and plaster.

In the end, the project memorializes years of history, admiration, friendship, and mutual respect.

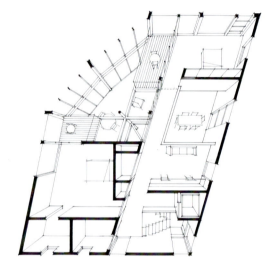

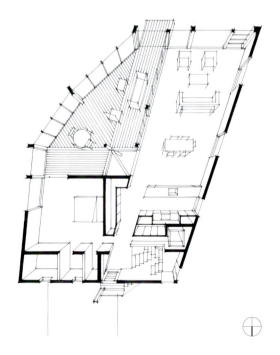

Top right Second-floor plan
Bottom right First-floor plan
Opposite Marsh façade

Above Street façade
Right Stairs to second-level entry
Opposite Entry façade

Above Double-height living and dining areas
Opposite Main living areas open to marsh and water vistas

Left Double-height screened porch
Opposite top View over main living space from home office on second-floor mezzanine
Opposite bottom left Stair detail
Opposite bottom right Exposed galvanized steel structure in double-height porch

McDaniel Marsh House

Chesapeake Bay House

Neavitt, Maryland
2011

There is a pool on top. So are all the exterior elements—decks, porches, terraces, and the mechanical systems.

The reason is simple. The site, a quiet cove in a waterman's village on Maryland's Eastern Shore, is subject to strict guidelines that protect the Chesapeake Bay. The allowable footprint for everything on the site—*everything*—is sized to the ruined foundations of a previous house, long gone but excavated, surveyed, and documented.

That house was about the size of a double-wide trailer, so now it is all piled up, all fitting on deck—like a modern ark with 1,664 square feet of interior space.

Given the height and the weight to be supported, the structure is made of cross-braced steel moment frames that impose themselves, and are celebrated, throughout the plan.

The open-plan first floor has multiple sliding doors, which turn the interior into a porch. A winding stair rises to two stacked bedrooms and continues to the rooftop pool.

On the exterior, white cedar shingles and stainless steel will weather naturally. There is no paint or stain on the outside.

The interior is all white.

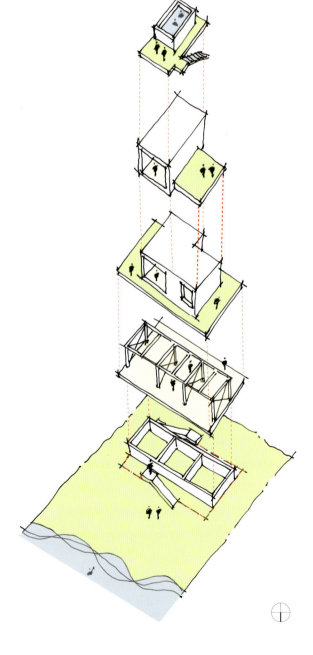

Right Stacked axonometric diagram
Opposite Chesapeake Bay façade

Above Living and dining areas open to water views
Opposite top left Second-floor bedroom
Opposite top right Stair detail
Opposite bottom View from kitchen

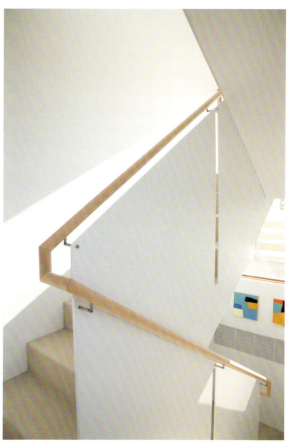

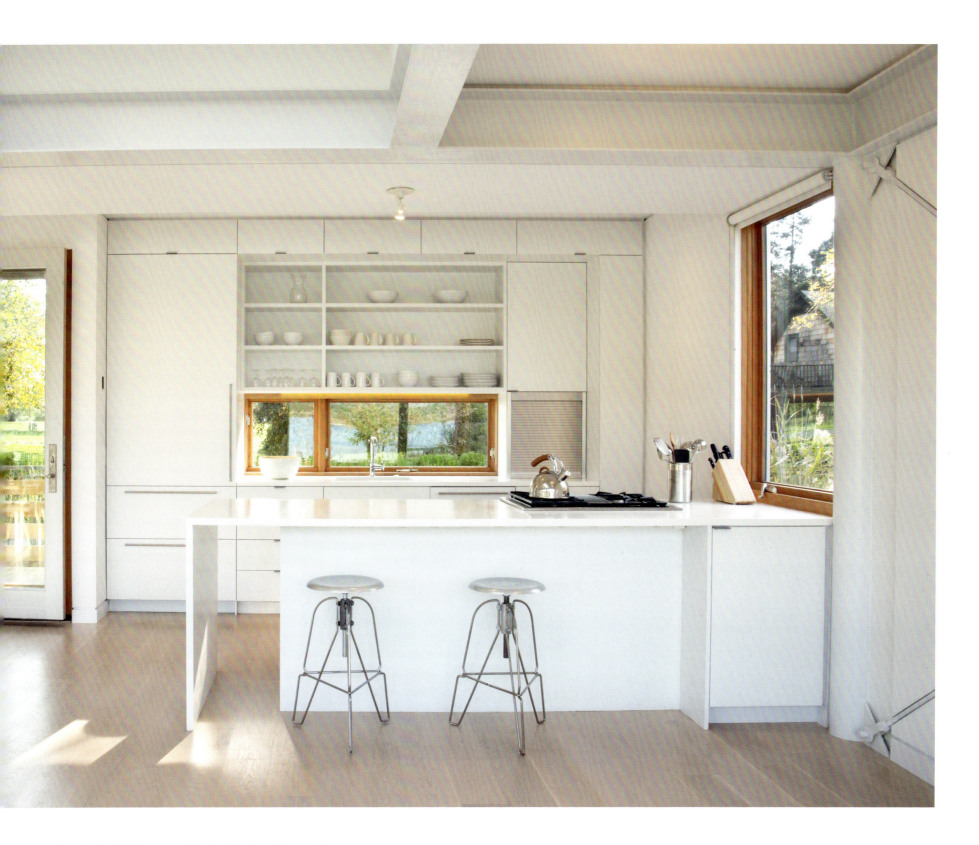

Opposite Desk with views through double-height slot to Chesapeake Bay
Above Kitchen and entry

Chesapeake Bay House

Right Rooftop pool
Below Dining area
Opposite Street façade

Reid Beach House

Bethany Beach, Delaware
2019

This Mid-Atlantic coastal house is designed to focus views and activity on the ocean while providing complete privacy from the neighboring houses, just 20 feet away.

To do this, two gabled forms shift forward and back to enclose a private ocean-facing deck and pool. Folding glass walls open the entire beachfront wall to this deck, pool, and the ocean beyond.

Within, an open stair and glass-enclosed elevator tie the three levels of the house together and continue to a roof deck with expansive views.

Top Entry elevation
Bottom Ocean elevation
Opposite Ocean façade at dusk

Left View from beach
Opposite top Rear terrace with pool and bridge over dunes to beach
Opposite bottom Section

Reid Beach House

Above A glass elevator separates the entry from the main living spaces
Right Second-floor office and double-height dining room open to ocean views
Opposite top Dining and living areas viewed from kitchen
Opposite bottom Kitchen

Reid Beach House

Singh Hoysted Live/Work

Bethesda, Maryland
2015

The program for this infill house in a close-in suburb of Washington, DC, includes a generous studio for an artist who works in mixed media. We were excited by the idea of a house and studio overlapping so that each part reveals itself to the other in multiple ways, interlocking home and work.

The house is conceived as a block, with one quadrant carved out to create a courtyard, resulting in an L-shaped plan. Like the rest of the house, where work and life are combined, the courtyard is part house and part outdoor studio space, allowing for dinner parties among the works in progress.

On the exterior, the parts of the house that conform to the block are white and have simply placed openings. The L-shaped courtyard walls are black shingles, with irregularly placed openings, as if to suggest that the creativity of the work in the studio is bursting out of the rationality of the house. Joining the live/work function is a stair rising through the house in half levels, with openings, large and small, that frame vistas as one moves between the house and studio.

Top right Second-floor plan
Bottom right First-floor plan
Opposite Entry façade

Above Courtyard is flanked by living and studio wings
Bottom left Balcony detail
Bottom right Studio window detail
Opposite Courtyard at dusk

Left A stair opens to, and links, the studio and residential wings of the house
Top left Double-height studio
Top right Stair with studio beyond
Bottom Living room

Top left View through stair
Left Concept diagram
Above Kitchen with stair and studio in background
Opposite Kitchen and dining

Rappahannock Bend Summer House

King George, Virginia
2009

Five years after renovating their historic country house, our clients asked us to add a new pool/guest house on the site of their existing pool. In the spirit of eighteenth-century farm dependencies and summer kitchens, we proposed to build a complete, largely open-air structure that could be used as a self-sufficient house during clement weather, a guest house year-round and a pool house in the summer.

An existing stone wall at the pool site is used to divide open-air public spaces from conditioned private spaces. A thin copper roof on white brick piers sails above, providing much needed shade on this exposed riverside site.

Below the roof, stucco masonry walls enclose the only conditioned spaces, a bathroom and a bedroom. Other services—kitchen, shower, mechanical and pool equipment—are outdoors, housed in timber-clad walls. Wood louvers provide additional sun control.

The layering of structure and skin, and their assembly, provides the architectural language for the project. The control of light and its play upon surfaces provides the sensibility. Throughout, this house attempts to revisit eighteenth-century concepts of comfort and sustainability in a twenty-first-century language.

Below Section
Below right Plan
Opposite Guest house and stair to roof deck

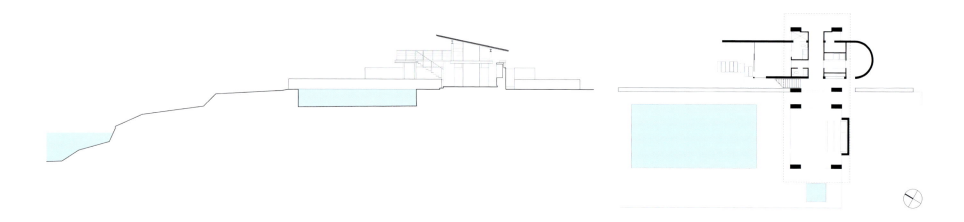

Opposite top Pool house and guest house at dusk
Opposite bottom left Entry elevation viewed from driveway
Opposite bottom right Views out over pool to river beyond
Right View from main house
Bottom Low stone wall separates guest house and pool

Ridge House

Little Washington, Virginia
2013

This project occupies an extraordinary location in the Blue Ridge Mountains of Virginia. The immediate site forms a kind of saddle, on the intersection of a ridge on the east–west axis and a valley running north to south.

The house runs along the ridge and bridges the valley, opening its long sides to the long north–south views. The pieces of the program—a two-bedroom house, screened porch, pool terrace, entry court, and garage—are articulated and aligned along the ridge axis. A continuous roof spans the entire collection, transforming the modest scale of the individual pieces into a unified composition over 200 feet long, carrying a single line across the entire façade. Only one space rises above the continuous roof, elevating a seating area for taking in distant views.

Like a bridge, the structural system is continuous and insistent. Steel frames at 16 feet on center march the length of the building, expressed inside and out. All exterior surfaces—windows, walls, and ceilings—are arranged in modular subdivisions of this structural bay.

Low-maintenance metal-and-fiber cement panels clad the exterior walls. Inside, white wall planes form a backdrop for nature outside, and the owners' art collection within.

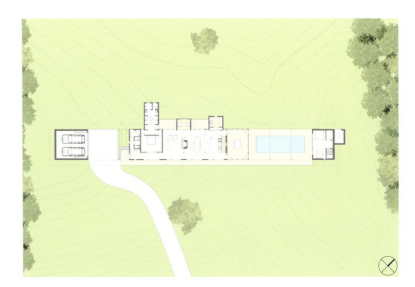

Top Plan
Above Elevation
Opposite Approach

Right Kitchen
Below Living with dining and kitchen beyond
Opposite top Pool deck connects studio and house
Opposite bottom left Model
Opposite bottom right View of house from studio

Ridge House

House on Tilghman Creek

Claiborne, Maryland
2017

Situated on a remarkable Chesapeake Bay site with water on three sides, this house occupies the exact footprint of a previous house that fell victim to fire and deterioration. The new house conforms precisely to the old foundations.

The house takes advantage of the constant breezes that cool the site. It opens fully all around, and folding glass walls can disappear entirely on the eastern face, directing the view to the largest expanse of water. When those walls open, recessed screens 10 feet beyond can drop to make the entire house into a screened porch. The result is a convertible house that allows for several degrees of enclosure depending on the weather: closed house/open porch, closed house/screened porch, open house/screened, or open entirely.

Motorized shades have been programmed to minimize solar heat gain in the summer while allowing adequate natural lighting. Substantial overhangs at two levels allow windows to be kept open; the use of AC is avoided except on the hottest and most humid days. Several mature trees close to the structure were successfully preserved, creating a shade canopy that helps with passive cooling. Geothermal wells provide heating through radiant floors, and 9,000 gallons of water collected from the roofs and stored in eleven large cisterns in the basement provide for most site irrigation needs. Strategically placed zinc-clad roof monitors—above the otherwise-shading overhanging roof—bring controlled daylight deep into the interior to balance natural light from the perimeter.

The natural beach and marsh areas were preserved and protected to mitigate against shoreline erosion and to encourage favorable conditions for terrapins and other fauna. About half of the lawn was converted into a meadow with native plants, grasses, and forbs (wildflowers), which helps reduce runoff from the property and the adjoining farmland. Emphasis has been placed on native plants for all new landscaping.

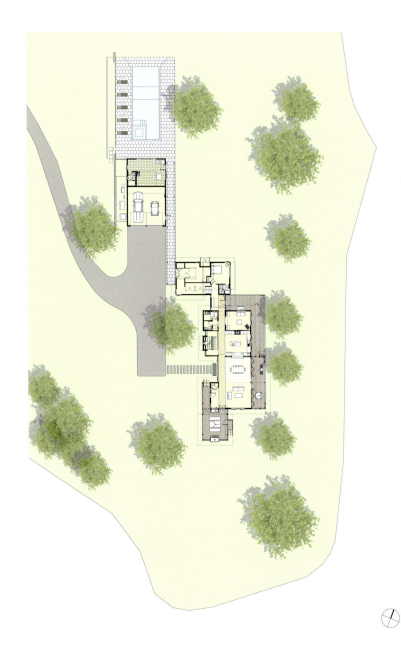

Above First-floor site plan
Opposite Open wooden screen divides the stair and kitchen

Left Entry façade
Top Aerial view of site
Above Entry façade at dusk; exterior colors and materials recede into the wooded site

House on Tilghman Creek   99

Opposite Double-height dining area viewed from bridge above

Above Folding glass walls open the main living areas to water views

Left Interior with window wall and screens retracted, fully open to outdoors

House on Tilghman Creek

Opposite top Entry court created between house and garage, separated by walkway to pool
Opposite bottom Entry elevation
Above Garage, guest house and pool house walls screen the pool from the driveway

House on Deep Creek Lake

Swanton, Maryland
2023

This house occupies a rustic lakeside site in western Maryland, replacing a collapsing log structure that was no longer habitable.

The new house is a simple row of spaces strung parallel to the lake shore, allowing each major space to take advantage of the natural lake and forest views. Modulating these spaces is a series of equally spaced structural steel frames, opening room to room, while wood-framed windows and doors open each room to the water.

The length of the house is split by the entry and stair, with the private principal bedroom and office on one side, and the common spaces and guest bedrooms on the other. On the exterior, darker colors and materials help the house to merge into the forest.

The project is under construction with completion expected in 2023.

Left First-floor site plan
Bottom left Side elevation
Bottom right Lake elevation
Opposite top Lake façade
Opposite bottom left Section
Opposite bottom right Interior view of main floor

Del Ray House

Bethesda, Maryland
2023

This new house, in a rapidly urbanizing close-in suburb of Washington, DC, replaces a 1950s house that had suffered too many additions and renovations to be coherent.

A centered entry splits the brick façade and opens directly through the house to the rear garden, with the major rooms on both floors distributed on either side of the central path.

The simple rectangular plan and massing gives way at the rear to two projecting volumes. One, the principal bedroom, reaches up through the roof, and the other, the guest room, extends out over the rear terrace.

The project is under construction with completion expected in 2023.

Top right Model
Right First-floor site plan
Opposite top Double-height dining room
Opposite bottom left Garden façade
Opposite bottom right Kitchen

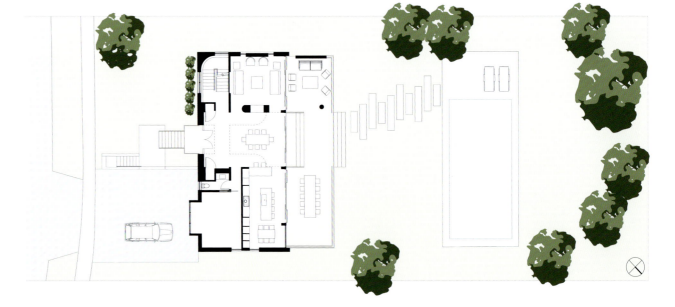

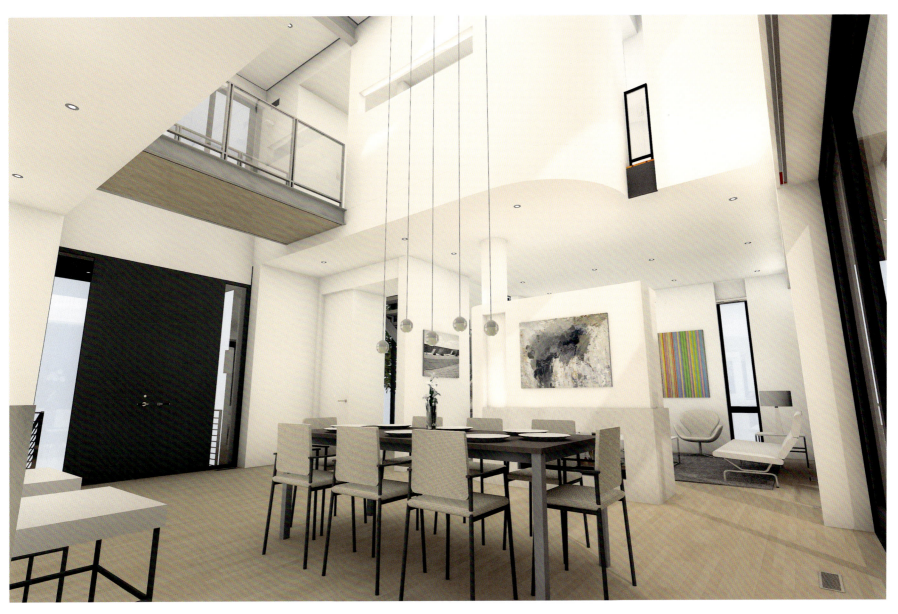

Multigenerational House in Jamaica

Jamaica
Design 2022

This new house in Jamaica will serve several generations and branches of a family whose roots are on the island.

Designed to sleep as many as fifteen people, the house is broken into alternating pavilions and gardens, creating a village-like composition of related structures. The pavilion gardens, and the porches and terraces beyond, fully integrate indoor and outdoor living, made possible by Jamaica's benign climate.

Taking advantage of the hillside slope, the main floor and terrace level overlook a host of group spaces for exercise and leisure activities. Local construction methods of white-painted concrete walls, stone tile floors, and exposed wood roof framing provide all the color and texture needed, blending with the 180-degree views as the site slopes down to meet the Caribbean Sea.

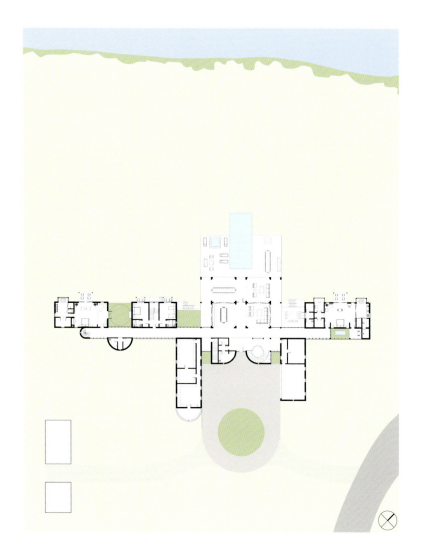

Above First-floor site plan
Opposite top Water elevation
Opposite bottom left Dining for extended family
Opposite bottom right Aerial view

Changed Houses

Live/Work

Montgomery County, Maryland
2019

This project is essentially a home office addition, albeit a large one, that accurately reflects the current needs of effectively combining work and home in the same location.

Wanting to spend more of their work hours close to family, an international couple, who each own their own businesses, asked us to provide private office spaces for each, as well as a shared conference room for teleconferences and lounge space for business-related social events.

At the end of an existing long driveway, a new parking court serves both house and office. Entry to the new office wing is via a bridge across a narrow weir. From there, a new lateral entry hall connects to the existing house via the kitchen at one end and terminates at a new stair connecting all three levels at the other end. Along the new hall is found access to porches and terraces that can be used by both the home and office.

Both spaces now overlook a new formal lawn that, in turn, opens to the forest and the Potomac River beyond.

Right Site plan
Opposite Entry to addition allows work and residential functions to be separated

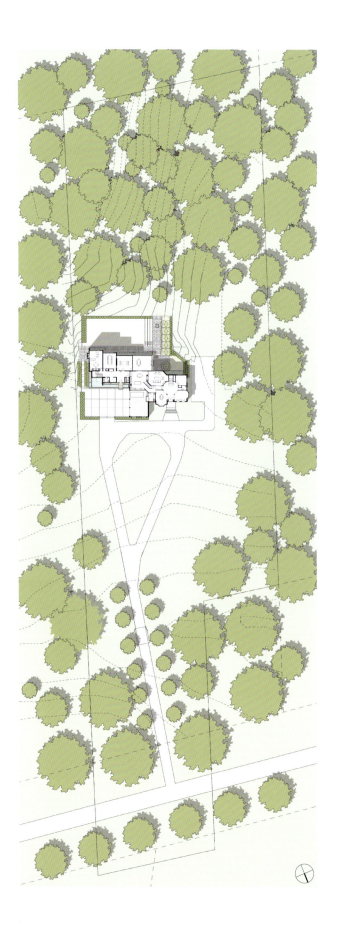

Left Work and lounge areas in the home office wing connect to a deck that is shared with the main residence
Top Conference room
Bottom Common areas of home office wing with entry beyond

Live/Work 115

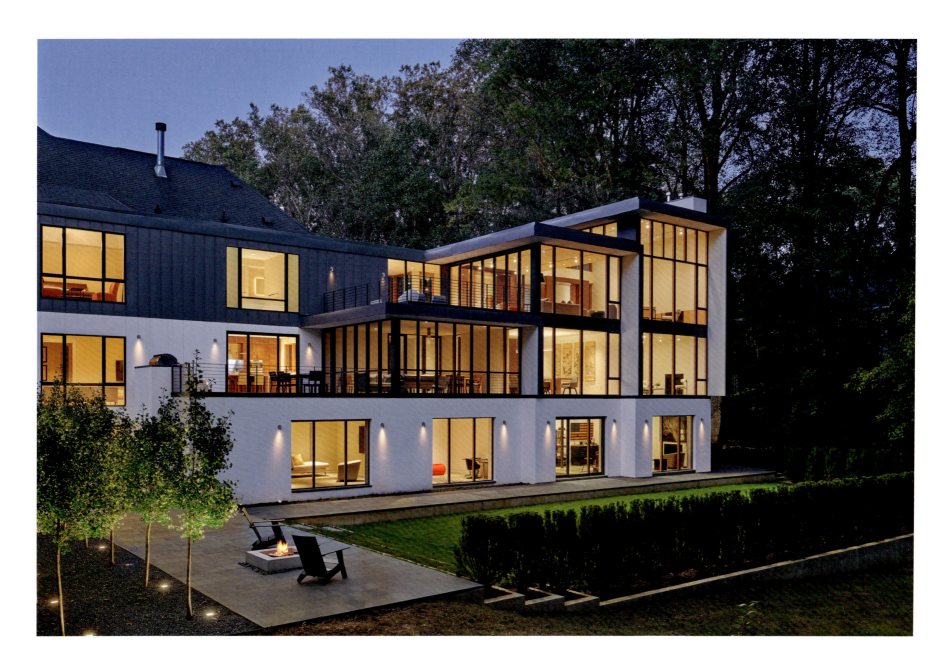

Opposite top left Work and residential functions overlap and connect through a series of shared decks
Opposite top right Entry and stair in the new office wing also connect through to the main house
Opposite bottom left Side elevation
Opposite bottom right View of terrace through new stair
Above Garden façade

Opposite East façade
Top left Entry stair from parking court
Top right Entry
Left Section

Live/Work 119

Georgian Modern

Washington, DC
2020

This project involves the complete renovation of an ample center hall Georgian house on a corner site in northwest Washington, DC.

Starting at the front door, a clumsy stair, completely blocking the through-hall, has been replaced with a highly crafted steel-and-wood stair and landings. These weave through the entire height of the three-story-plus basement house. Each landing along the way hovers in a new stair tower at every level, allowing the occupants to simultaneously feel a projected connection with the gardens.

The design of the stair sets the materials for the entire house, where curved wood panels and built-in cabinets delineate a series of connected but discrete rooms. Extending to the exterior, similar geometries executed in white brick and bluestone negotiate level changes on the site and create another series of connected but discrete outdoor rooms. With the existing brick of the house painted white, and new exterior wall surfaces clad in black standing-seam metal, this reductive palette has been used to weave new and old together.

Between inside and out, a porch near the kitchen can be opened, via folding glass doors, to the interior. Screens drop from the ceiling when needed. At the other end of the house, a former sunroom has been opened to the living room and the fireplace now serves both spaces.

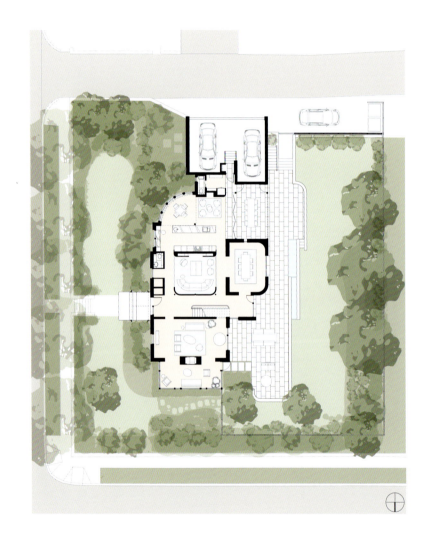

Above First-floor site plan
Opposite Garden terrace with kitchen beyond

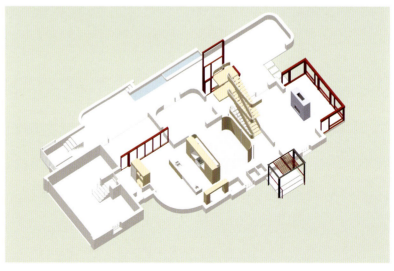

Opposite top Kitchen
Opposite bottom Axonometric diagram
Above left and right Stair detail

Above Stair
Right View of skylight at top of stair hall
Opposite top Garden elevation
Opposite bottom left Entry façade
Opposite bottom right Garden terraces

Georgian Modern

Woodmont 17th Floor

Bethesda, Maryland
2021

Our clients are the first owners of a seventeenth-floor three-bedroom unit in a new condominium building in the evolving downtown of Bethesda, Maryland.

Once a sleepy two-story commercial area surrounded by suburban housing, Bethesda has, following the construction of the Metro just blocks away, emerged as a lively walkable urban center.

Our clients, who resided in a neighborhood of largely single-family houses in Washington, DC, were ready to move to a denser urban environment with easy access to public amenities. While their new residence had a well-organized floor plan and featured a 40-foot-long wall of windows overlooking the surrounding community, it was developed and detailed with all the charm and finesse of an ordinary developer apartment block. Our clients wanted more, and better, materials and detailing, and ample space to display art, as one of the clients had recently closed her commercial gallery and kept all of her favorite works to feature in the new space.

The architectural solution to all of this was to make one large cabinet of white oak and blackened steel that touches all of the main rooms—living, dining, kitchen, family room, and entry—and which transforms in treatment and layout as it moves from space to space. In it are bookshelves, art walls, sliding doors, and parts of the kitchen.

In the remainder of the apartment, the same palette of white oak and blackened steel is also used to create custom-designed desks and storage units in the bedrooms and offices.

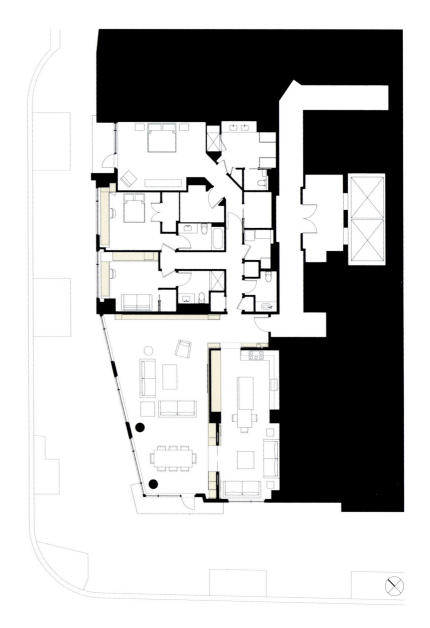

Above Plan
Opposite View from entry

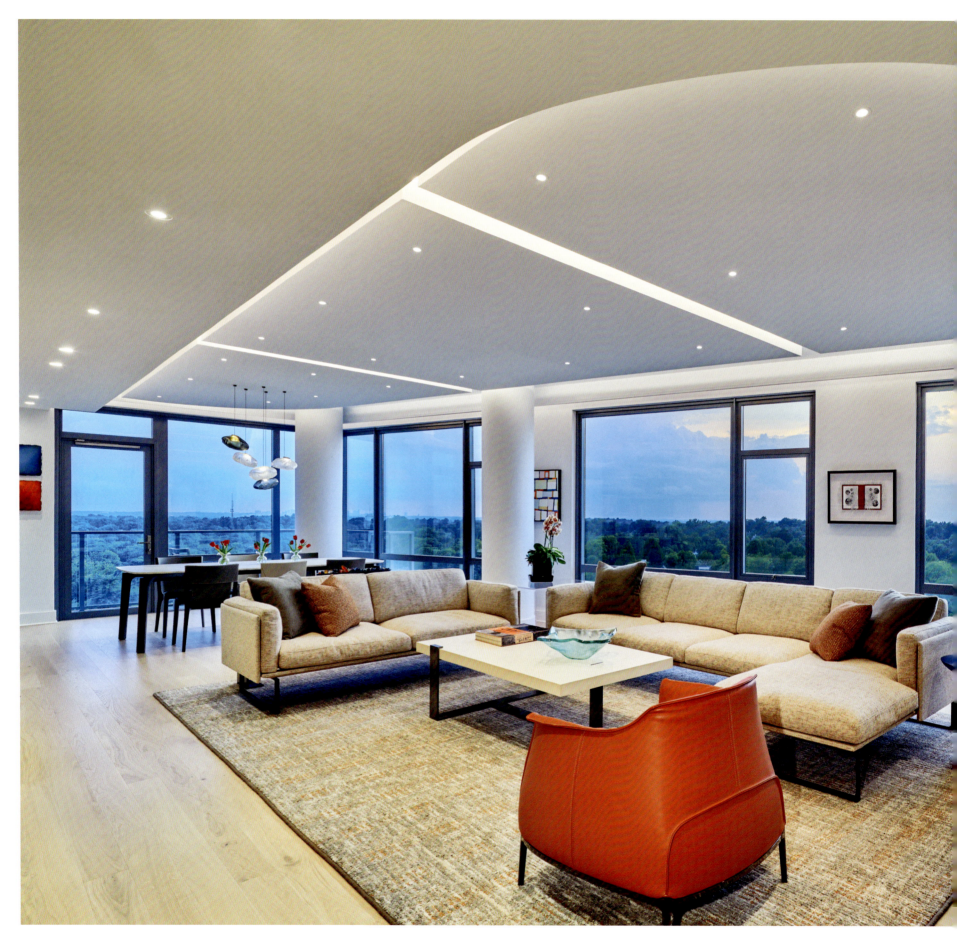

Left Living and dining areas open to city views
Top Living room
Bottom Perforated sliding door separates entry and kitchen

Woodmont 17th Floor

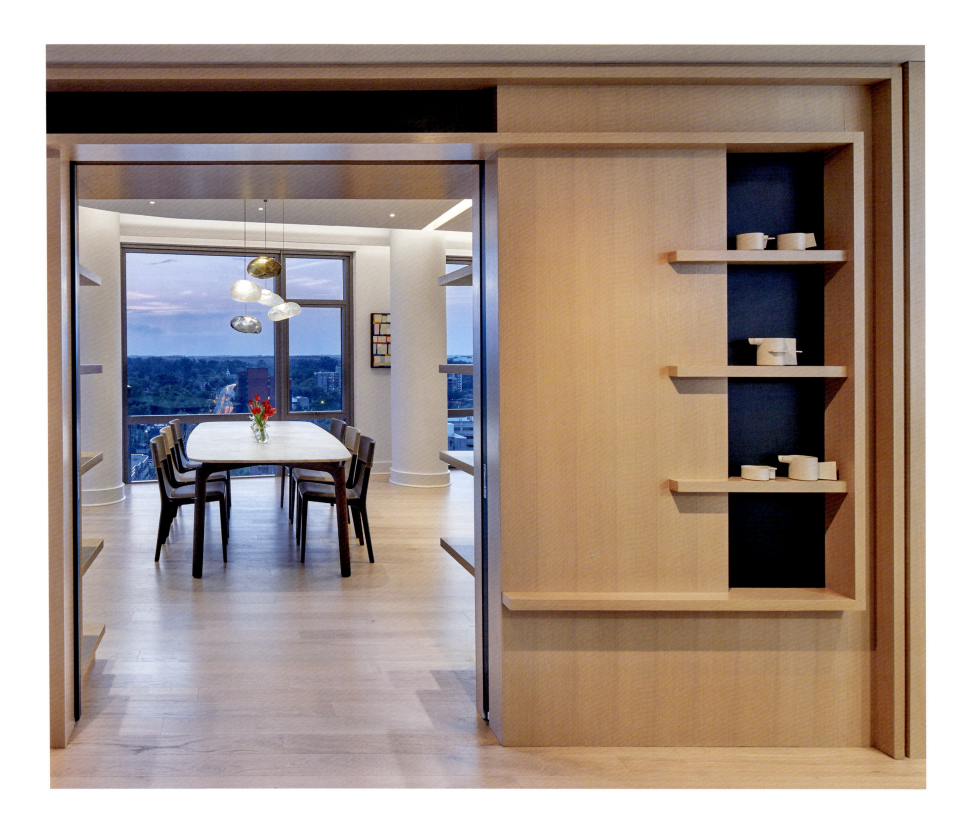

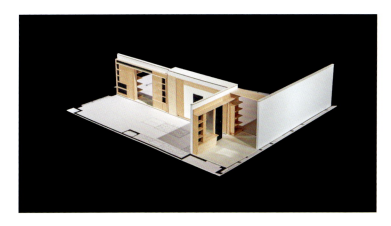

Opposite Dining viewed from kitchen seating area
Top Model, entry side
Above Model, living room side
Top right Kitchen
Bottom right Home office

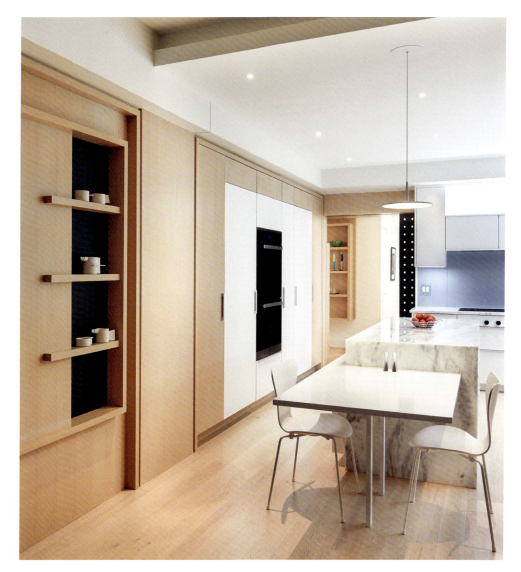

Woodmont 17th Floor

ADU Crestwood

Washington, DC
2021

When is an Accessory Dwelling Unit (ADU) also an in-law suite and a guest wing? This project was designed to work as all three. Our clients asked us to design an addition that could function as a suite for aging parents, an ADU for a future owner, and a possible guest room for the existing house. They also asked that it not invade an unusually ample backyard in this close-in Washington, DC, community, known for its diversity, trees, and adjacency to Rock Creek Park.

Pushing the long, thin mass of the addition to one side and toward the back of the yard allowed space for family activities and sufficient privacy for the in-laws. Due to both zoning regulations and program, it is connected to the house by a glazed bridge/gallery, lifted off the ground to protect the roots of a mature oak tree.

The first floor of the addition can be accessed from both a rear alley and the existing house, each with separate entries. A second-floor guest room with its own door and interior stair can function either on its own, as part of the house for guests, or for the in-law suite should a caregiver be necessary. The resident father-in-law, a retired mechanical engineer, worked with us to design a state-of-the-art mechanical system. Radiant floor heating and a high-efficiency air-to-water heat-pump system with energy-recovery ventilators operate within a highly insulated and sealed thermal envelope to minimize energy use and maximize thermal comfort without the use of carbon sources.

A single-pitched roof both refers, and defers, to the existing house and is designed to support a future array of solar panels. Throughout, careful detailing, simple surfaces, and ample views create interior spaces that live larger than they actually are.

Top right Axonometric diagram
Right Section
Opposite Addition viewed from house

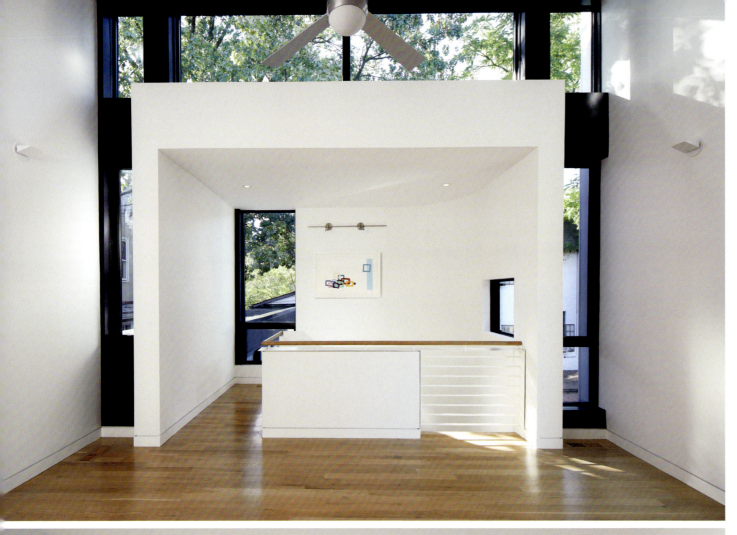

Left Stair connects the second-floor bedroom with the first-floor living area

Bottom left First-floor living area

Opposite top New unit connects to the main house via a glass gallery

Opposite bottom left Stair

Opposite bottom right Gallery connects the house and accessory dwelling unit

ADU Crestwood

Truss House

Bethesda, Maryland
2021

Spec-built developer houses of the last few decades are frequently built the same way—exterior bearing walls supporting long-span, gang-nailed roof trusses, eliminating the need for intermediate bearing walls and allowing partition walls to be placed as desired.

In this case, that meant that three separate rooms—living, dining, and kitchen, along with a small hallway—could all be easily combined into one generous space, accommodating all functions. With dividing walls now removed, the expansive continuous rear wall allows a series of large sliding glass doors, all opening to the garden beyond.

However, a room of that generous size cannot work proportionally with the standard eight-foot ceiling height found in the typical developer house.

The solution lay in the trusses. While the original builder never intended them to be seen, these lightweight, stick-framed elements of some delicacy are spaced evenly along the length of the house. They have now been revealed in strategic locations, with the plan organized to work with their rhythmic spacing. The trusses, cleaned up and painted, support skylights in key locations, providing height, light, and overhead filigree, overcoming the height limitations of the original interiors.

Colors were selected from the work of the much-admired African American Gee's Bend quilt makers of rural Alabama, connecting the interiors to a part of the cultural heritage of the family.

 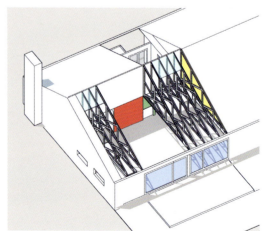

Above left Section perspective
Above right Axonometric diagram with trusses
Opposite New skylight over now-exposed trusses brings daylight deep into the living area

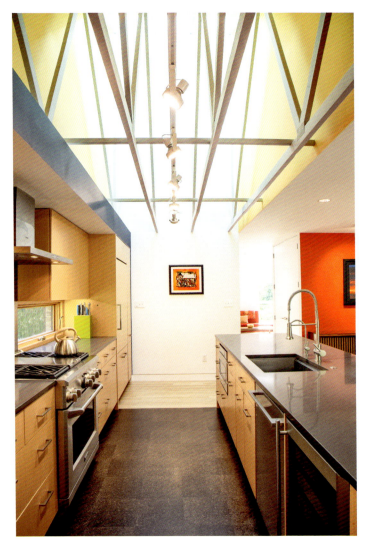

Above Kitchen

Right Bold colors define the living spaces

Opposite top A wall of custom cabinetry anchors the living area

Opposite bottom left View of entry and living area from the dining table, each defined by a bold color

Opposite bottom right Large sliding glass doors open living, dining, and kitchen to the garden

Truss House

Woodley Park House & Garden

Washington, DC
2018

This elegant early-twentieth-century house had been renovated before, but had never been made to connect to its site in any way, a connection made difficult by the tightness of the urban site and its compound slopes and steep topography.

Our client asked for a new kitchen, a screened porch, and a series of outdoor spaces, including gardens and terraces, with a fireplace and a pool, all within these limits. Working from the outside in, the design began by fitting the pool and terrace into the rocky, sloped rear yard, completely filling the space. The interior responded to that landscape with a renovated kitchen at the terrace level and a screened porch above.

The excellent traditional formal rooms of the existing house remain and the center hall is extended through to the garden, incorporating the new kitchen as it passes along the way. Here, the ceiling goes up into a complex cubist cross-section and the extended center hall stair arrives at a new second-floor screened porch overlooking the garden. Directly outside the kitchen door is a small terrace with a fireplace embedded into the end of a raised pool, allowing the flames to serve both the terrace and the kitchen. A second upper terrace runs alongside the pool and faces south.

The challenges of the tightness of the site and its topography led to a complex interlocking arrangement of interior spaces and exterior gardens and terraces, all in a tiny footprint that accounts for every square inch.

Right First-floor site plan
Opposite Garden, pool, and terraces viewed from kitchen

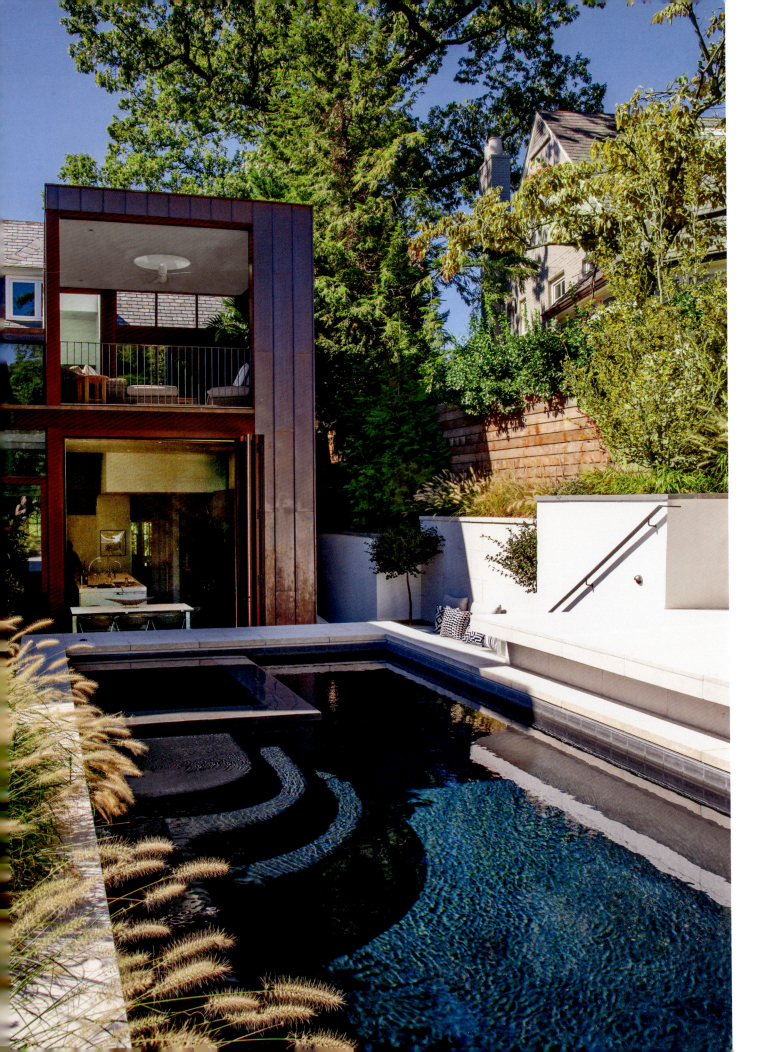

Left Folding window wall opens the new kitchen to the pool and garden terraces

Opposite top left New addition is topped by a second-floor porch with retractable screens

Opposite top right View of garden from second-floor porch

Opposite bottom Section

Woodley Park House & Garden   143

Opposite Family room opens to the new kitchen

Above Modern black extension of the existing stair rises over the new kitchen, leading to a new second-floor porch above

Left Stair detail

Porter Street House

Washington, DC
2015

This project involved the first-floor renovation of a modest postwar house in the historic Cleveland Park neighborhood of Washington, DC.

Keeping within the existing footprint, every interior wall was removed. Where divisions were desired—between entry and living space or between kitchen and dining—it was accomplished with walls of built-in cabinetry, made of American white oak. Existing interior perimeter walls of this first floor are white-painted plaster.

A new kitchen opens to the living/dining area, which itself opens to views of a new, delicately detailed stainless-steel and wood stair at the entry.

Finally, a new folding glass wall opens the rear wall of the house, expanding the interior to the garden beyond.

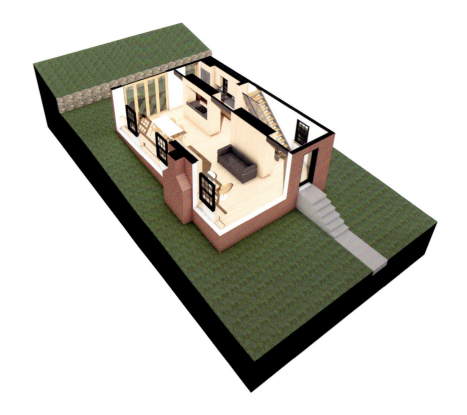

Above Axonometric diagram
Opposite Walls of custom cabinetry define the spaces in the now-open plan

Above Folding wall of windows opens the main level to the garden
Opposite top Now-open views from dining area to kitchen and entry
Opposite bottom left and right Details of new stainless-steel and wood stair

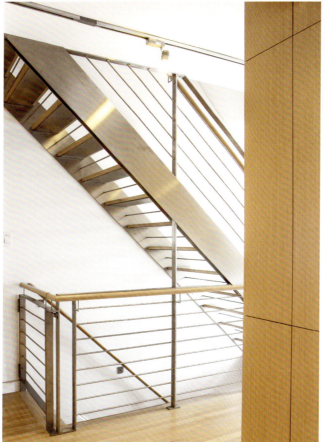

House on Maxmore Creek

Royal Oak, Maryland
2018

At just over 200 feet long, this 1950s Chesapeake Bay waterfront rambler had, over time, rambled a little too far.

Additions on additions had stretched the program far too much for it to have any sense of place or any kind of compositional power. So, when our clients asked for two new offices and some renovations, we proposed a tower, more or less in the center. Partly, because making a big difference in one surgically located place did not require renovating the whole house or rambling any farther. Partly, because getting up 15 feet, or 25 feet, or, ultimately, to a roof deck 40 feet above the ground is a powerful way to experience the beautiful but flat landscape of the bay's eastern shore. And, partly, because making a stair that goes all the way up is a fun way to move around and to bring in light.

Finally, the entire house was reclad in white cedar shingles, helping it all play together happily.

Below Section through tower
Opposite Walls of windows and a roof deck face the water

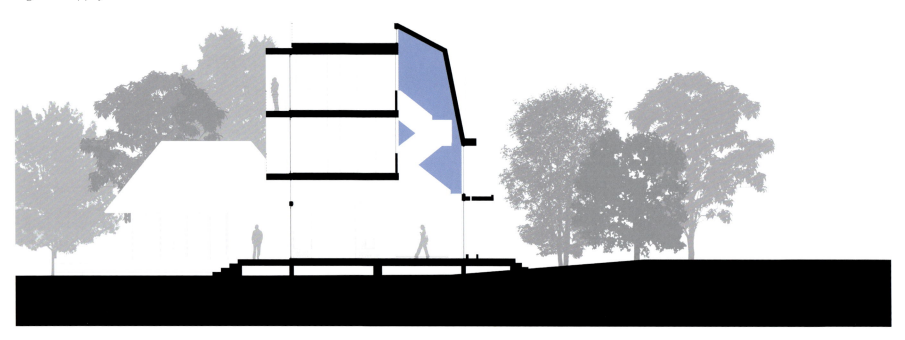

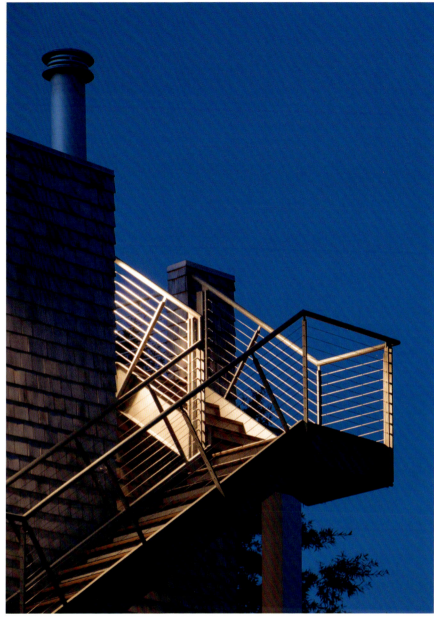

Opposite Street façade
Top left Entry on lower level of new tower
Above Stair to roof deck
Left Waterfront elevation

House on Maxmore Creek

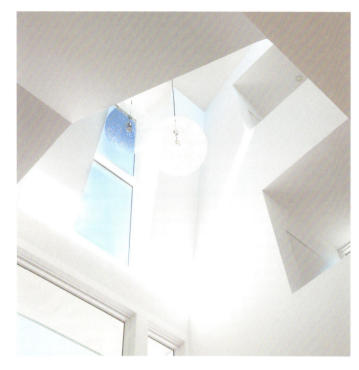

Opposite top left Folded planes of new skylight over entry and stair
Opposite right New stair and entry viewed from living room
Opposite bottom left New open stair connects the three levels of the tower
Above Living area opens to water views

21st Century Cabin

Highland, Maryland
2016

Built for a NASA engineer, a cellist, and their small child, this project involves the renovation of and addition to a modest 1,200-square-foot cabin—their primary, and only, residence—in rural Maryland.

The only additions were a spiral stair replacing a ladder to the existing loft and a proper entry, with closets. New built-ins provide the additional storage needed for an everyday minimalist life.

The owners, in a nod to their cultural heritage, asked for a house with no furniture other than a small movable table for eating while seated on the floor. Two sleeping mats are rolled up and put away during the day. This lack of specific uses for rooms allows the entire house to be opened during the day through the use of multiple pocket doors, or closed up at night to create two private bedrooms.

The entire house can be heated with a small wood stove, which burns fallen tree logs and branches found on the site.

The original cabin has been clad in black asphalt shingles and the new additions in white stucco.

In keeping with the family's efforts to live lightly on the land, a sheep and two goats, black and white, now graze to keep the meadow trimmed. The guest house is an Airstream trailer.

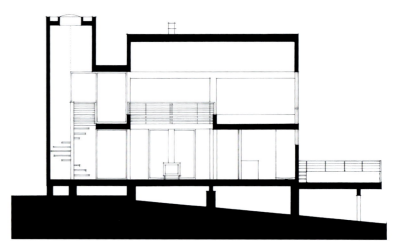

Top Section
Bottom Model
Opposite Addition of a white stucco entry/stair tower opens up the original tiny cabin

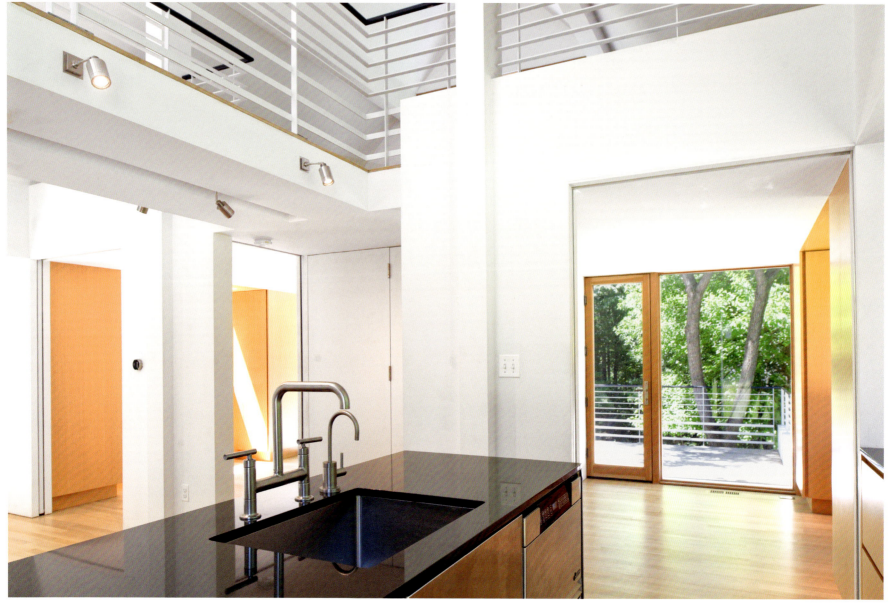

Opposite top left First-floor daytime configuration, with sleeping mats stored and bedrooms open

Opposite top right First-floor sleeping configuration, with doors closed for privacy

Opposite bottom Double-height kitchen with views to mezzanine above and deck outside

Right View into new entry/stair and open living area

Above The rural site, opening to meadow in front and woods surrounds
Opposite left Bridge and stair from mezzanine
Opposite top right Detail of new spiral stair
Opposite bottom right Skylight above stair

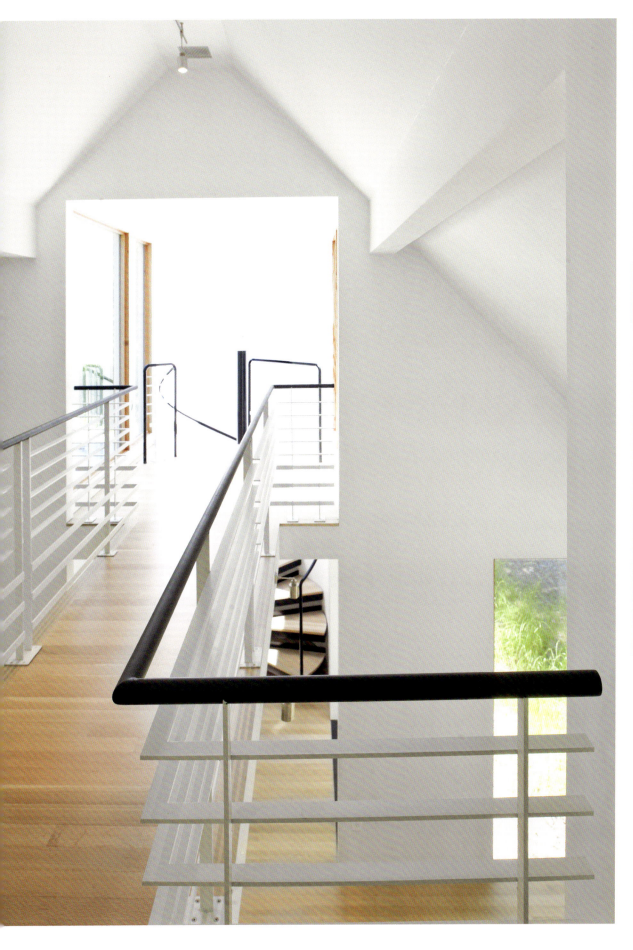

21st Century Cabin **161**

Georgetown House

Washington, DC
2018

The third time is a charm.

Sited on a Georgetown bluff overlooking the Potomac River and Francis Scott Key Bridge, this house has, arguably, the best view of any house in the city. It has had three owners over the last twenty years, and we have worked with each one of them.

For the first client, we renovated the rear 15 feet of the house—which had been a bad, and structurally failing, addition to the original nineteenth-century townhouse. A new four-story steel-and-glass curtain wall opened up the interiors to views of the river. A new kitchen and minor interior renovations were carried out at the same time. The second client took us to the top to create a roof deck that added an outdoor component, creating ringside seats to an amazing view.

The current owners redid everything not done by their predecessors. The interior of the original townhouse was gutted and modestly reconfigured, and every surface replaced. Central to this is a new, very carefully detailed stair that enlarged and replaced the original old, tight winders, and connects all levels, both functionally and, now, architecturally.

Finally, the interior finishes from the first renovation were transformed from black steel and maple millwork to a luminous white, completing with paint the total transformation of the house without adding a single square foot.

Above Plans
Opposite New stair in entry brings delicacy and light into the formerly dark space

Above Central living room opens to double-height seating area with expansive views of the city
Right Section perspective
Opposite Double-height seating area overlooks Georgetown and the Potomac River

Above left Double-height seating area viewed from the third-floor bridge

Above right First-floor kitchen and dining room with double-height seating area above, viewed from the rear deck

Opposite Fourth-floor primary suite provides extensive views over the Potomac River. Recessed motorized shades drop for privacy.

Left Dining room viewed from kitchen
Bottom left Kitchen
Opposite top Dining room with stair leading to double-height seating area above
Opposite bottom left and right Stair details

Georgetown House

Ranleigh Road Library

Arlington, Virginia
2018

To connect and separate. As people live longer, and endeavor to engage socially as well, and as long as possible, a style of elder housing is evolving and being reinvented as parents move back to again share accommodations with their now adult children. Add this to the numbers of professionals working from home, and a new model for integrating life, work, and family has appeared.

In the recent past that might have incorporated the spare bedroom, but more clients now request space to work from home, as well as a self-contained unit, connected to but separate from the main house, and designed to be fully accessible. Often this element is considered in conjunction with a larger architectural project, fully integrating the rewards of being with extended family with other new components—in this case, a library for 12,000 books as a home office.

On a steep site, an original large, gloomy porte-cochère spanned the drive to join a good rustic midcentury house to a separate one-story garage and adjoining small guest room. This ground-level room was enlarged and fitted out as a self-sufficient apartment, with a small terrace, for a retired college professor. Above it is the library for the political science scholar husband, currently writing a multivolume history of American foreign policy—a task expected to last many years. Accommodating his research needs and his collection required lining the room, the stairs, and a small passage between them with book shelves—even spanning overhead as one enters the space. Here, books do make the room.

Finally, the porte-cochère connecting house to addition was carved away to still provide cover between buildings and cars below, but to let significantly more light into the drive, the apartment, and its entry.

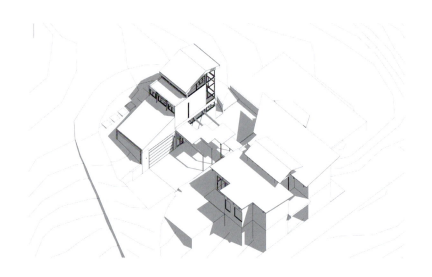

Top Axonometric diagram of library addition and its connection to the main house
Bottom Section
Opposite Books completely line the library, extending to the wall of the entry stair beyond

Left Corner slot window integrated with bookcases brings light and views into the space

Opposite top Large corner window provides sunny seating and views to the house beyond

Opposite bottom left Entry elevation from the driveway

Opposite bottom right View of the library from the garden

Ranleigh Road Library

Hutner Porch & Pool

Chevy Chase, Maryland
2016

Twenty years after we renovated our clients' Chevy Chase rambler, we were asked back to design their retirement present to themselves—a swimming pool and a screened porch.

On this hilly site, the only flat ground dictated that the pool be located immediately behind the house. The result is a slender band of water, running the full width of the house, with a screened porch for shade at one end and a terrace for sun at the other.

The screened porch is an exercise in dappled sun and carpentry. It is supported on steel legs that continue, partially clad in wood, to the roof, where corresponding beams cross over the top. These are exposed to view and make the roof a fifth façade, visible from the second-story primary bedroom.

The façade facing the pool has two doors, one on each side of the water. In the center, a retractable screen opens the pavilion directly to the water, allowing the occupants to dive from the interior straight into the pool.

Construction involved two pages of 11-inch by 17-inch working drawings and an extraordinary carpenter.

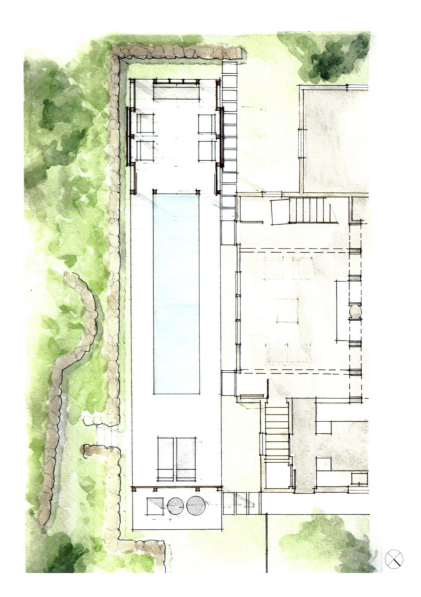

Above Plan showing connection to existing house
Opposite Porch and pool viewed from hillside garden

Left With screen retracted, porch connects directly to the pool
Opposite top View from porch along length of the pool
Opposite bottom left View of porch from garden gate
Opposite bottom right Wooden wall slats create ever-changing shadow patterns

Hutner Porch & Pool

Opposite top Wooden wall slats diffuse the sun's rays, creating dappled light to blend the porch structure into the garden

Opposite bottom left Porch detail

Opposite bottom middle Detail of steel pool structure with cross bracing

Opposite bottom right Pool detail

Left View into porch with screen retracted

López Forastier-Hellmann House

Chevy Chase, Maryland
2018

The renovation of a 1950s split-level added space without increasing the footprint, going up and back, while maintaining, on an established street, the low scale of the existing front façade.

To link the entry garden directly to the rear yard—a connection prevented in the original house by the stepped half-level cross section—a new front-to-back slice is carved through the house, and a new stair unifies every level as it winds up, down, and through the structure. It ends at a new upper-level primary bedroom suite, bringing light through a south-facing dormer, flooding both new and existing areas with light.

The house continues to present a modest single-story face to the street while now rising under a continuous metal roof to towering volumes in the garden.

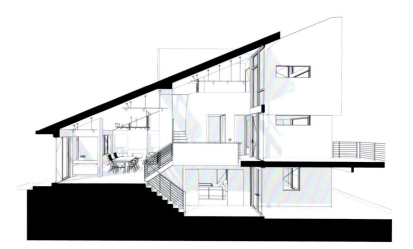

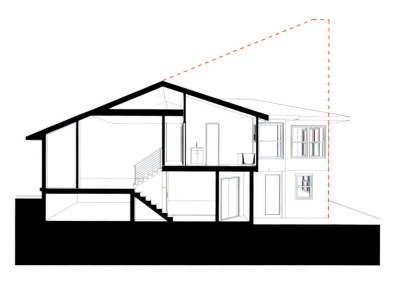

Top Section
Bottom Section (before)
Opposite Garden façade

Above New dining area with seating beyond
Right Kitchen
Opposite Open stair connects all levels and opens to the rear garden

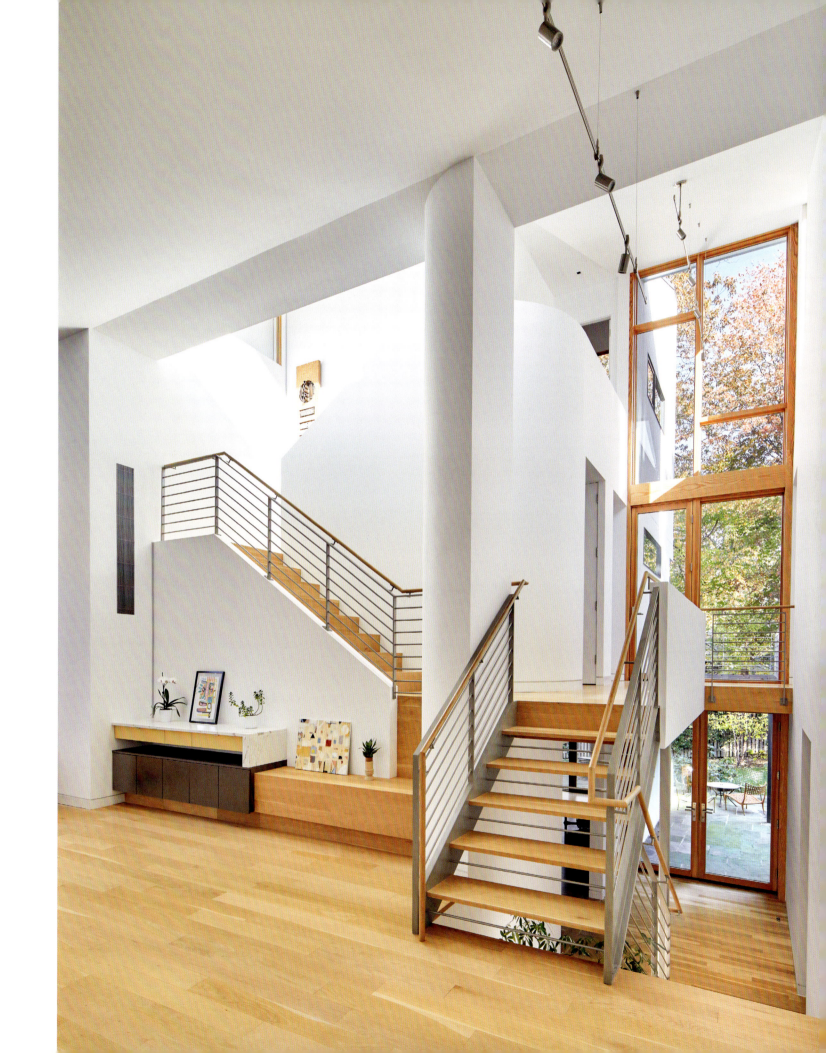

Edmund Street House

Washington, DC
2017

This renovation/addition opens up the interior of a charming but claustrophobic 1940s traditional house.

The first-floor spaces are no longer separated by walls and doors but by freestanding elements—closet, powder room, and stair, which allow longer and richer vistas both within and out to the garden.

As the wall for the television was removed, a lifting device now comes up from the rear of the kitchen counter to allow viewing on demand.

On the second floor a new primary bath floats over the first-floor garden room addition.

Throughout, the modesty of the original house is preserved in both scale and impact, even while connecting the interior to the garden in a much more direct way.

Above Model

Opposite Addition provides a porch and a series of decks overlooking the garden, as well as new interior space

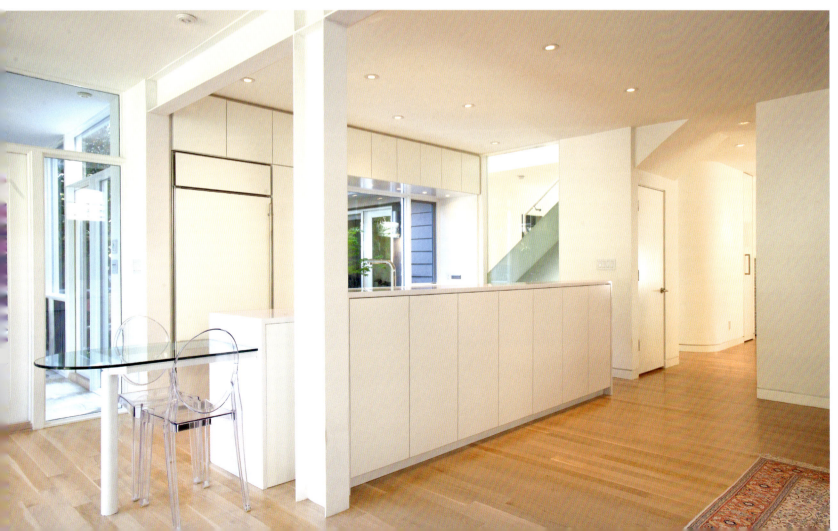

Opposite top The open kitchen and living room connect to the rear garden

Opposite bottom A glass wall between the stair and kitchen brings light into the center of the house

Left Open stair viewed from entry

Below Garden façade

Edmund Street House

House in Kenwood

Bethesda, Maryland
2016

This house, in one of Washington's close-in suburbs, was renovated in the late 1970s by Washington architect Hugh Newell Jacobsen. The timeless quality of Jacobsen's work has held up well, but the primary bedroom suite had not been an important part of the original work and the new owners approached us to update that part of the house.

In the new plan, the original bedroom has been left as a sitting area within a suite that is now enlarged. The bedroom proper moved to a small addition above a rebuilt first-floor porch, allowing for higher ceilings and larger windows. The baths and closets were gutted and reconfigured to create a spa-like ambiance.

The detailing, proportions, and quality of light pay respect to the Jacobsen aesthetic. Fittings, lighting, and hardware were updated to current standards and technology, but otherwise the difference between the new and old is seamless, and undertaken with great restraint and respect.

Above Second-floor plan
Opposite Steel bookshelves in sitting area flank the entrance to the bedroom

Opposite top left Primary bath

Opposite top right Seating around fireplace in primary bedroom suite

Opposite bottom Louvers provide privacy for the bed nook

Right Extension of the bedroom suite over the porch provided space below for a new garden terrace

House on Poplar Avenue

Takoma Park, Maryland
2013

This project converts a tiny midcentury modern house into a small modern one. What had been a one-story box on a walk-out basement is now a two-story modern box on a walk-out lower level.

While simple and economical in construction—straight-forward framing, no new footings or foundations—the three small original bedrooms have moved up and out of the main level, freeing up much-needed space for a reconfigured, generous open plan for the living, dining, and kitchen.

As the client is one of the area's most accomplished builders and served as contractor, we were able to selectively indulge in highly crafted elements, such as specialized cabinetry and an articulated stair. A simple exterior shape now gives way to an interior of surprising richness and complexity.

On the exterior, a simple black metal form is elaborated with a series of colorful attachments. A two-story projected window bay, an entry canopy, and frames for window groupings are all in colors inspired by Richard Diebenkorn's *Ocean Park* series.

Above Main floor plan
Opposite View from street

Left Sloped site allows three full levels to face the wooded garden
Opposite top left Living and dining viewed from stair landing
Opposite top right Bridge from street to entry accommodates the sloped site
Opposite bottom left Custom console in the entry matches the kitchen cabinetry
Opposite bottom right Open-plan living room and kitchen viewed from dining area

House on Poplar Avenue

43rd Street Townhouse

Washington, DC
2017

This started with a truly ordinary Developer Colonial townhouse condo whose amorphic floor plan featured small rooms with a variety of ad hoc boxy intrusions for stairs, fireplace, powder room, and HVAC chases—not ideal for the display of the client's considerable collection of art glass.

As much as possible was erased. In the short direction, the dividing line between kitchen and dining room was removed and one large loft-like space was created. We chose the simple strategy of connecting the dots of the unmovable bumps to create continuous curving lines along the opposing long walls. These fluid edges are defined by carved-in niches, creating shelves for the display of the glass and by illuminated soffits above. Front and back walls and windows could not be altered.

The vibrant colors of the art now pop in the clean white space.

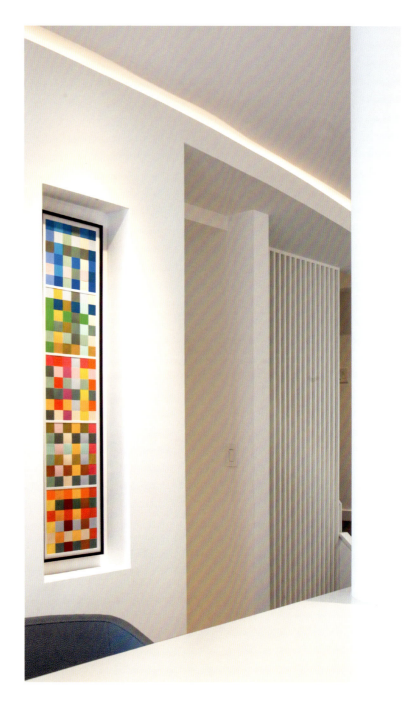

Right View over kitchen island to screen that divides the stair from the now open plan
Opposite top Curved walls running the length of the space provide display areas for art glass
Opposite bottom left Detail of illuminated niches in curved walls
Opposite bottom right Axonometric diagram

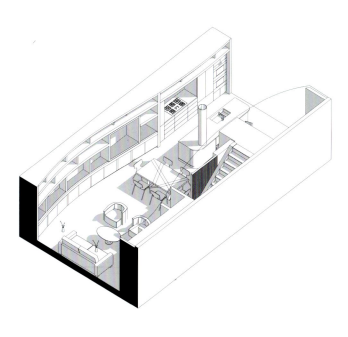

43rd Street Townhouse

Xia Yang House

McLean, Virginia
2023

Two of the original three parts of this existing 1970s house, the living areas and the garage, are to be removed and replaced, while the third, the sleeping areas, remains with some renovations.

The new living areas and garage are configured on the site in a way that creates outdoors spaces, serving the living areas and offices on both the approach and the forest sides.

The resulting long composition steps up the hill toward the entrance, reminiscent of a small Greek village.

The project is under construction with completion expected in 2023.

Above Axonometric diagram
Opposite top Entry façade
Opposite bottom left Interior rendering of main living spaces
Opposite bottom right middle Window walls extend the views into the garden
Opposite bottom right Kitchen

Not Houses

Greencourt Innovation Center

Rockville, Maryland
2017

The Greencourt Innovation Center is a catalyst in the redevelopment of an existing warehouse district in Rockville, Maryland, guided by the Twinbrook Sector Plan, which identifies the area as a new technology hub for the county.

Three existing warehouses built sequentially in the early 1960s have been modified and added to, creating an environment for innovation in technology.

The site is a through-block parcel, fronting on two streets. It drops in elevation across the site by one full story, from a courtyard and lobby on the east side to the larger court and lobby on the west. A slot through the building connects both lobbies, and open vertical circulation further supports interaction among the building's tenants.

The existing masonry and precast concrete structures have been retained, revealed, and highlighted, and supplemented with a new exposed steel-framed third floor. Within the larger lobby, the elevator, a major stair, and two suspended conference rooms energize the space with visible activity.

The project has received LEED Gold Core & Shell v2009 certification. Key sustainable features include the significant reuse of existing structures, the walkability to nearby metro and alternate transportation measures, optimized energy performance, and a 20,000-square-foot vegetated roof.

In its role as a catalyst for the redeveloping neighborhood, the building strikes a balance between recalling the past of the warehouse district and looking forward to a new future of technology and innovation.

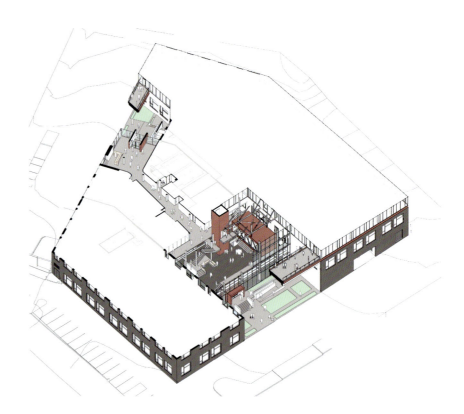

Above Diagram of double lobbies and major circulation through the building
Opposite West lobby with elevator tower and suspended conference rooms

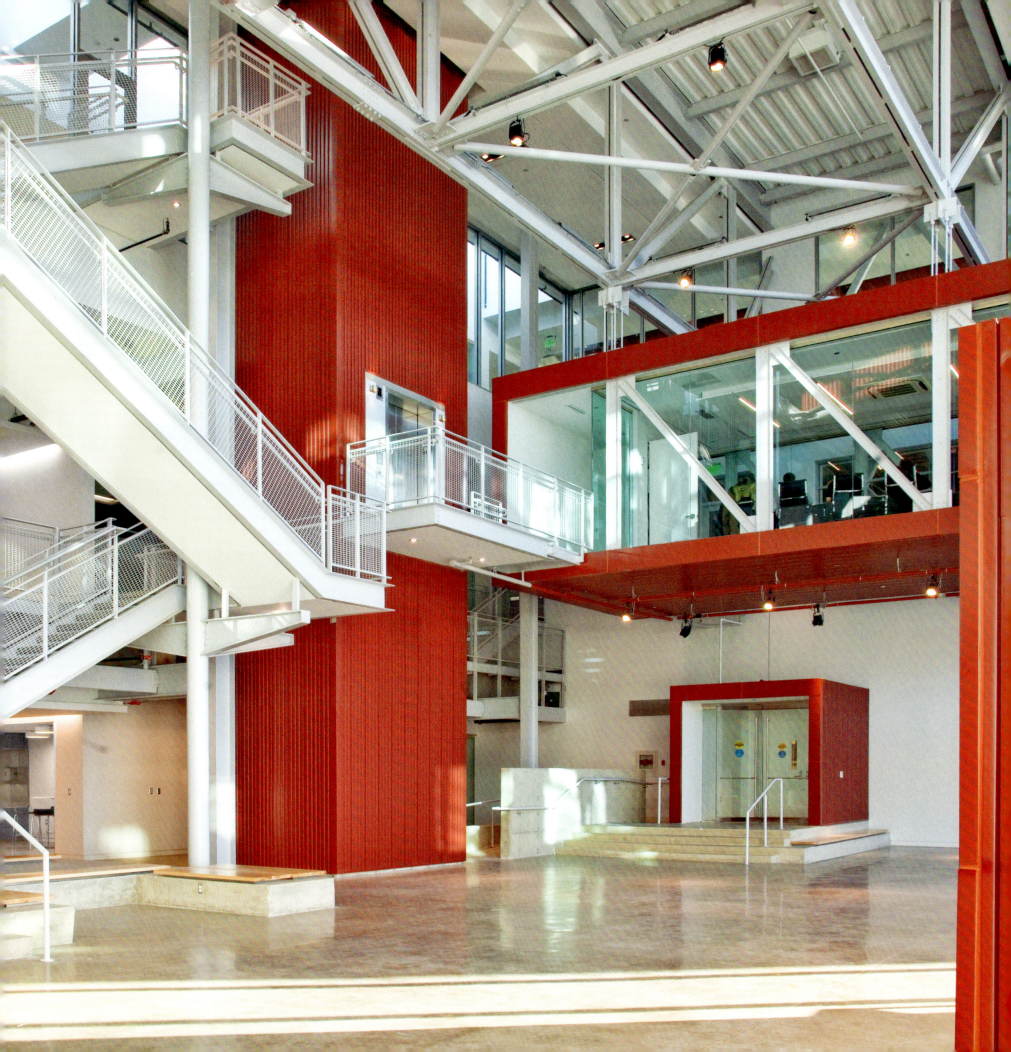

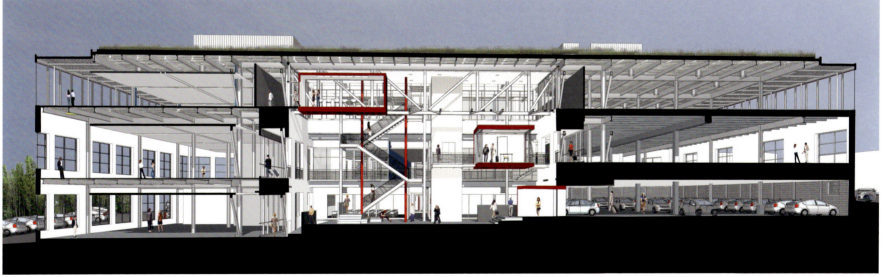

Opposite Entrance to west lobby
Top West lobby viewed from street
Bottom Section through west lobby flanked by tenant spaces

Greencourt Innovation Center

Above Entrance to east lobby
Right East elevation
Opposite East lobby

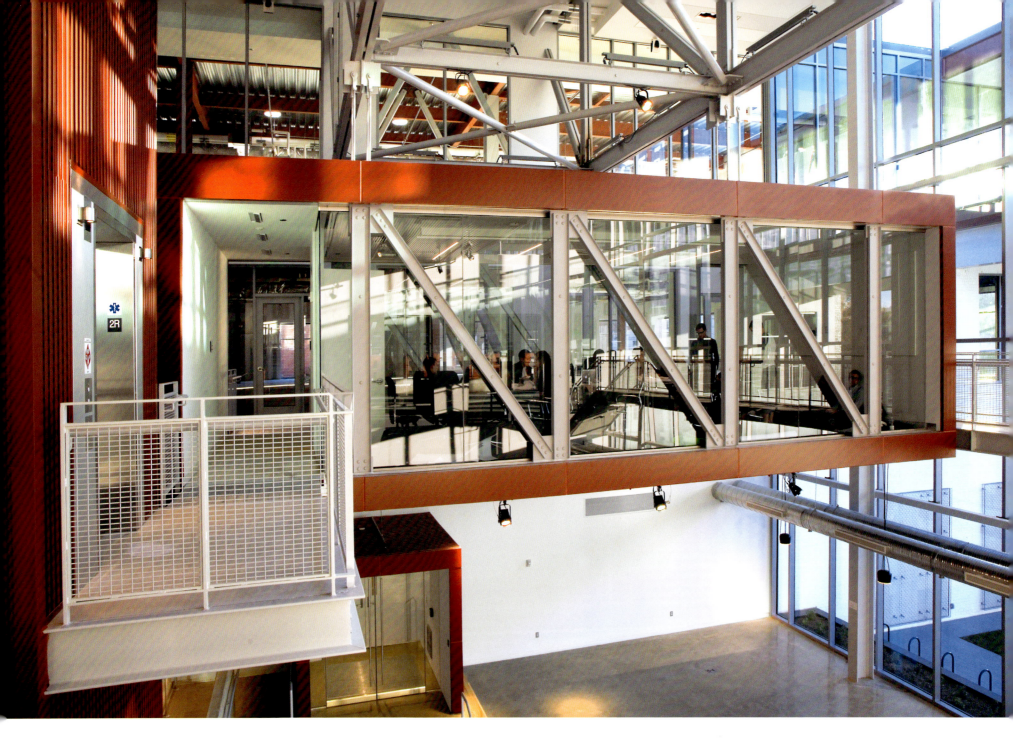

Above Suspended conference room in west lobby
Opposite top West lobby with suspended conference room and circulation bridges across west façade
Opposite bottom View from upper-level bridge down to west entry

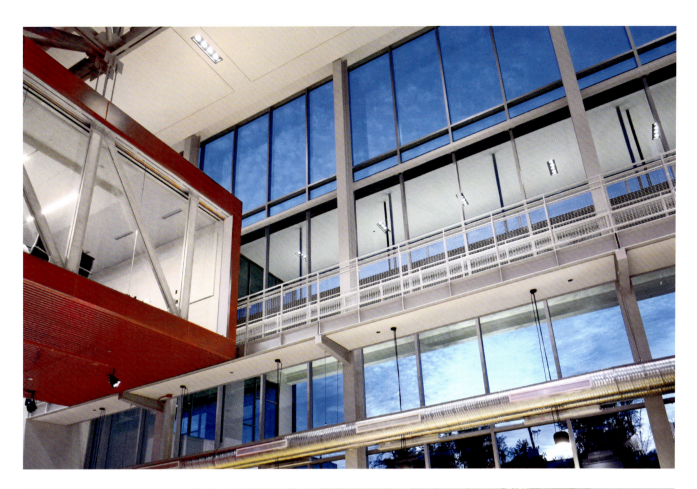

Greencourt Innovation Center

Opposite Circulation slot connects east and west lobbies

Right Elevator and stair create a vertical circulation core in west lobby

Bottom Tenant spaces overlook west lobby

Parker Metal

Baltimore, Maryland
2018

Built and occupied between 1923 and 1996, the Parker Metal Decorating Company building is a series of six one-, two-, and three-story masonry buildings in a formerly industrial area of Baltimore.

Baltimore's canning industry, and its need for decorated metal cans, is long gone, and finding a new use for the building, while preserving it, was a priority for the city. These new uses now include office and showroom spaces as well as a venue for events, performance and celebrations, all complementing the transitioning urban context around the site.

The project is completely surrounded by elevated freeways, train tracks, and existing parking lots. As the site has parking on two opposite sides, it was quickly realized that two entries connected by a long gallery-like passage was needed, leading to a centrally located hub with stair and elevator access to all three floors.

Aside from carving out both the long passage and the lobby spaces for circulation, very little reorganization was needed to convert from canning to twenty-first-century work and entertainment spaces.

Existing surfaces are left raw and complemented with new unfinished wood and steel elements. Throughout, the robust original construction is made visible and the history and configuration of the original warehouse structures are made legible.

Right Early concept diagram of major circulation paths
Opposite Curved hall connects two public entrances

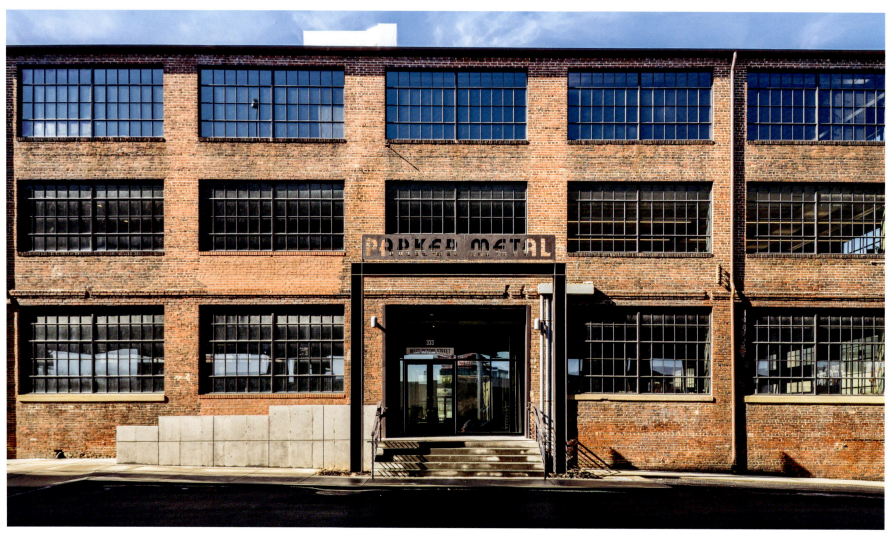

Opposite top East entry façade
Opposite bottom City views from tenant space
Above West entrance reflects the industrial origins of the structures

Left Stair/elevator lobby
Opposite top left Second-floor balcony overlooks stair lobby
Opposite top middle Second-floor balcony projects into lobby space
Opposite top right Openings through brick walls connect the two public entrances and the stair/elevator lobby
Opposite bottom Section

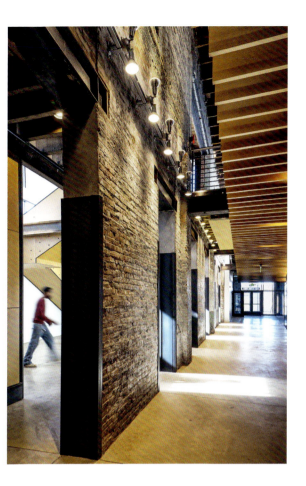

Parker Metal

Urban Courtyard Apartments

Washington, DC
2018

We were asked to design an eight-unit apartment building, composed of two to four bedroom units, targeted to DC's young urban singles. The premise that the city was the true living and dining room was embraced. With an eye to that, the number of bedrooms, most with en-suite bath, was to be maximized, and the common living spaces were to be airy, efficient, and smaller in size.

The site fronts onto a street of historic townhouses and has alleys both side and rear. We quickly realized that maximizing the by-rights footprint would also allow open space somewhere in the program. Rather than putting this in the rear, we chose to locate it in the middle, as a courtyard, creating an outdoor room for use by all of the residents. The courtyard also helps to break down the bulk of the building on the alley side, which could have been overbearing to the single-family townhouses opposite, and allowed the units to have light on three sides.

All units are connected by a central hall and stair that overlooks the courtyard, so the sense of community fostered by the courtyard is central to the experience of all of the residents in their day-to-day comings and goings.

On the street, the rhythm of adjacent townhouses influenced the massing of the façade. The two alley elevations are also treated as architecturally important, in acknowledgment of urban pedestrian circulation patterns. The required Green Area Ratio was achieved through a system of planters in front, rear, and along the courtyard, and a vegetated green roof. Bike lockers are provided in the basement.

The central metal stair was commissioned as part of VisionDC's first Art Tank, a nonprofit program aimed at encouraging economic development through, and within, the creative community.

Above Plan at courtyard level
Opposite View of second-story courtyard from side alley

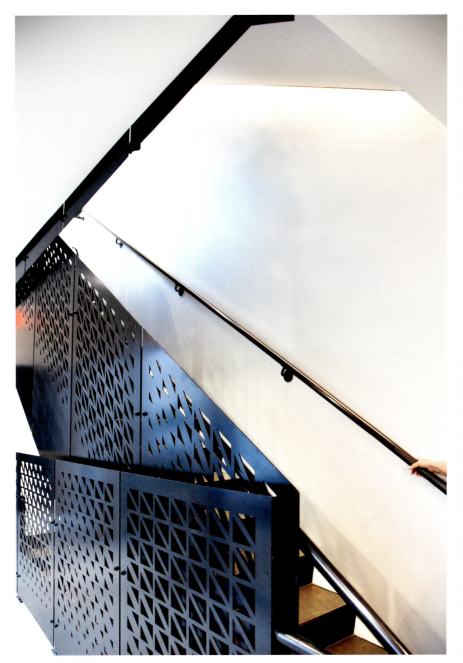

Opposite Apartment stacks front and back, connected by the stair hall, create an internal courtyard serving all residents
Top left Custom stair by Hiroshi Jacobs connects all levels
Top right View from roof into courtyard
Above Elevations (left to right): street; side alley into courtyard; rear alley

Above left Bay window overlooks street views
Above right Street façade
Opposite Rear façade

Watergate East Lobbies

Washington, DC
2019

Designed by noted postwar Italian architect Luigi Moretti, the design for the Watergate complex began in 1960. The first building, Watergate East, was dedicated in 1965. The complex was one of Washington's most iconic addresses even before the notorious 1972 break-in. Sited on a prominent bend in the Potomac River, the curvilinear geometry takes as much from the natural river landscape as it does from Pierre Charles L'Enfant's classic city plan.

The six-building/six-owner, mixed-use complex has three residential buildings, each with their own lobbies. We were asked to renovate the public spaces of Watergate East, a co-op with split lobbies on Virginia Avenue that flank and bookend the main entry to the site and its center public courtyard.

Multiple lobby renovations had occurred over the years. While limited to the existing lobby footprints, we sought to reconnect and reconfigure the lobbies to the exterior of the buildings through geometry, materials, and lighting, and to bring them back to the spirit of the original. The surviving Moretti details were preserved and in some cases extended, while new detailing involves sleek materials, fabrication, and new technology Moretti surely would have embraced.

The signature terrazzo floors have been restored, and are now complemented by a palette of curved Corian walls, mahogany cabinets, bronze mailboxes, and marble slab desks and wall panels, capped by a polished white Venetian plaster ceiling. Accommodations of other needs not known in Moretti's time, such as whole rooms for storage of Amazon deliveries and current technology for office and security staff, are incorporated.

These two important lobbies that flank the main entrance to the complex are once again an extension of the fluid architectural language Moretti planned almost seventy years ago.

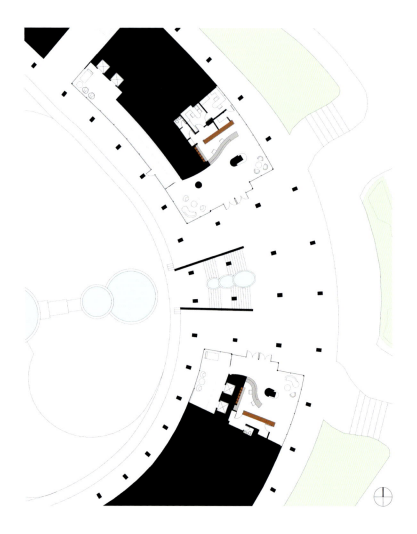

Above Street-level plan with main entrance into Watergate complex separating North and South lobbies
Opposite North lobby reception desk

Above North lobby facing Virginia Avenue

Right Axonometric diagram of North lobby with staff offices beyond

Opposite View over the complex's central courtyard to split lobbies and main entrance into site

Watergate East Lobbies

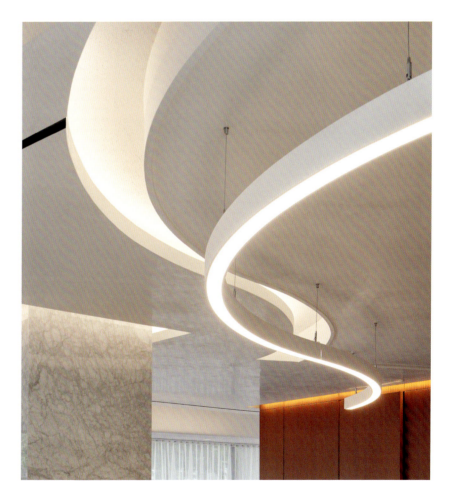

Left South lobby

Top Axonometric diagram of South reception and elevator lobbies

Above Detail of custom pendants over reception desk

Watergate East Lobbies

Opposite top North lobby finishes include original terrazzo, marble, Corian, mahogany, and bronze

Opposite bottom left North lobby facing Virginia Avenue

Opposite bottom right Slots of light in curved Corian walls take cues from the arrangement of the original exterior balconies

Right Polished plaster ceilings and terrazzo floors reflect light, recalling the Potomac River, which the Watergate complex overlooks

The Writer's Center

Bethesda, Maryland
2014 Phase 1
2019 Phase 2

The Bethesda Youth Center was designed in the 1960s by the young firm of Keyes Lethbridge & Condon, who went on to play a major role in the modern development of the Washington area. The Montgomery County–owned venue provided the local teen community with classes and social activities. Closed in 1970, the building spiraled downward, serving a variety of uses but chronically poorly maintained.

This midcentury modern building, leased from the county, now serves as the Writer's Center. The nonprofit community-centered organization is dedicated to the creation of an independent home for the literary arts, nurturing writing talent, and celebrating writers through classes, workshops, publications, and readings.

The building was renovated in two phases. The first phase reorganized the lower level, a basement with one line of high windows. Largely uninhabitable spaces were recaptured, asbestos abated, and offices and classrooms were reconfigured, brightened, and rejuvenated. Spaces were made ADA compliant in preparation for the second phase, which would make the building fully accessible.

The new plan allowed space for additional classrooms and the creation of a Writer's Studio, where local writers can rent private work stations. Daylight is maximized throughout by taking advantage of the windows along the original service ramp; glass walls in the classrooms extend the natural light into the formerly windowless spaces. Douglas fir woodwork and punches of vivid color further enliven what still is, but no longer feels like, a basement level.

The second phase renovated the front of house and the front of building. Beginning at the sidewalk, the building was made accessible and welcoming in equal measure. A porch/ramp/stair assembly was layered on to the existing facade, playing off the original structure in a lighter vocabulary.

Within, a new lift provides access to the lower level, the entry is opened up, the reception and office areas reconfigured.

Above Bird's-eye view of new entry and lobby configuration
Opposite Reconfigured entry is opened up, creating a bolder and more generous street presence

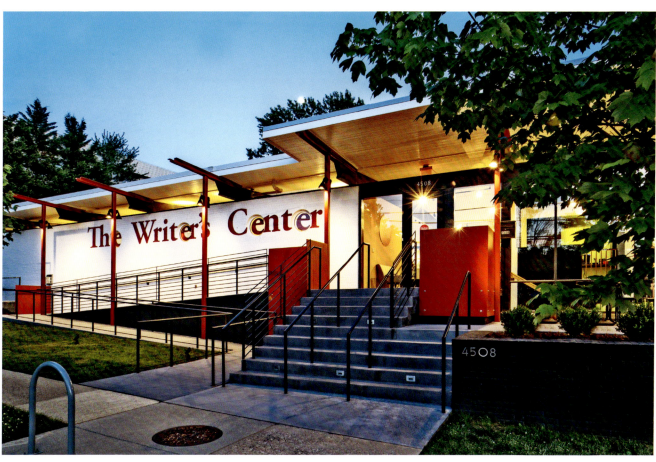

Opposite top Light and color refresh the newly reorganized lobby and office space

Opposite bottom Lower-level Writer's Studio

Left Large interior window walls bring natural light into the formerly dark classrooms

Bottom New ramp and stair structure is overlaid on the original building, celebrating the entry and making the building fully accessible

Politics and Prose

Washington, DC
2018

The Politics and Prose bookstore is one of the preeminent independent bookstores in America, a major center for the literary and political communities in Washington, DC, and a neighborhood hangout. Established in 1984, the bookstore is known for the depth of its offerings as well as an extensive calendar of classes and events, with daily author readings and talks. The popular lower-level café serves both the neighborhood and patrons. The existing store occupied three retail bays of a typical early to mid-twentieth-century commercial building on Connecticut Avenue. The thriving store, needing additional space, had annexed a fourth bay, vacated by a drycleaner.

Our objectives were to serve three needs: to renovate the existing coffee shop, to build out office space for the store's fifty employees, and to provide additional retail space for the bookstore. In all three program spaces, the owners asked that the new work build on the existing ethic of the store—comfortable, welcoming, and modest.

Opening to the parking area behind the building, the coffee shop, now The Den & Wine Bar, was stripped to its bare walls and structure, and all existing surfaces were left exposed. An adjacent staffroom was incorporated into the seating area, and connections to the kitchen were improved.

Also opening to the alley parking, the offices utilize the changes in grade of the site from front to back to provide two stories of mixed open and closed work spaces. New windows to the rear and a skylit atrium bring light into what had been a dungeon-like drycleaner's shop.

Finally, the new bookstore bay extends but improves on the aesthetic of the existing shop—tin ceilings, cherry shelves, and new display tables—to create a library-like atmosphere.

Above Perspective view of new café and offices
Opposite Staff offices

Above The building was stripped down to its most basic surfaces, with removed materials used and repurposed to provide finishes for the new volumes

Right Bridge connecting the second-floor offices crosses a double-height staff common area

Opposite top Wood structures salvaged during demolition of the old space are repurposed as finishing materials for the new construction

Opposite bottom left and right Work stations are not standardized but are configured in varying degrees of openness or privacy based on need and circumstance

Politics and Prose

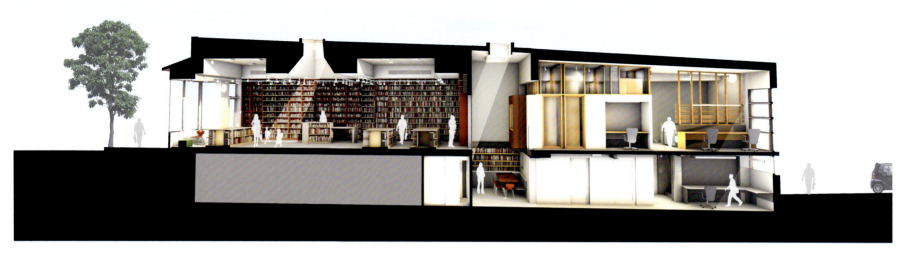

Opposite top Section

Opposite bottom Lower-level café

Above An interior window allows a second-floor office to overlook the skylit double-height common area and provides the spaces with much-needed natural light

Politics and Prose

Art Works Now

Hyattsville, Maryland
2017

Art Works Now is a nonprofit arts education organization in Hyattsville, Maryland, committed to community and to reducing economic barriers to participation in the visual arts. Through programs for students ranging from toddlers to elders, AWN brings arts education and creative opportunities to an underserved population in a developing middle- and lower-income community.

After years of occupying, and finally outgrowing, a rented facility in nearby Mount Rainier, Art Works secured a derelict flower shop on US Route 1, adjacent to the Hyattsville Arts District. Director Barbara Johnson was able to create an economic synergy when she brought in Ruth Gresser—her life partner and owner of the successful Pizza Paradiso group of restaurants—to take nearly half of the building for a new, much-welcomed restaurant in a community underserved in both pizza and art.

The new Art Works space preserves the 1950s roadside store/flower shop building, while renovating the already gutted interior for new studios and a gallery, with offices on a partly expanded, and now accessible, second floor. The existing building is now part of an energetic and colorful collage of new and old additions intended to create a cultural landmark in this strip of repair shops and used-car dealers.

Having already designed a house for the clients, this was a labor of love for the design team, as it was for all involved, from legal counsel to general contractor. The new facility is an architectural expression of this, and of the excitement generated within by the creative work spilling out the door.

Route 1 is better for this project, as is the Hyattsville Arts District, and as is this community who needs and deserves a place to discover and develop their creative lives. Art and pizza—win/win.

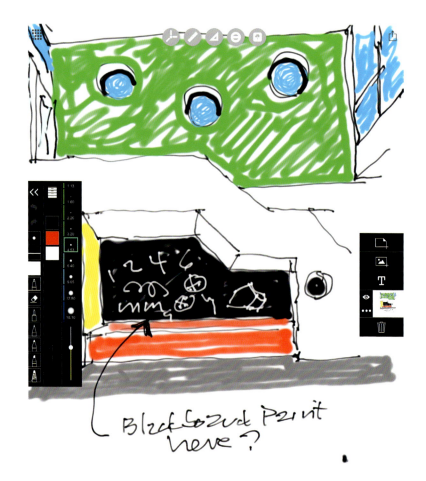

Above Concept sketch of stair hall

Opposite Bold forms and colors energize the entry hall and stair space, which serves as the central connection to all the activities throughout the building

Above Street view

Right Gallery

Opposite left A niche for coat hooks and storage bins is carved out under the stairway

Opposite top right Sign over street entrance

Opposite bottom right The entry stair hall connects all spaces, serving as lobby, gallery, circulation, and town square

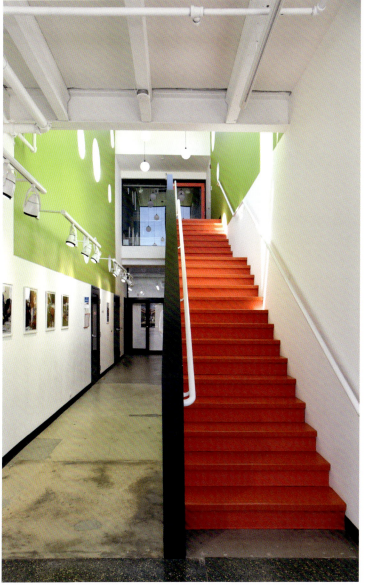

Art Works Now

Georgetown Mixed-Use

Washington, DC
2022

This mixed-use project involves four historic buildings and an equal amount of new construction in the heart of Washington, DC's historic Georgetown neighborhood.

The nineteenth-century structures front on Wisconsin Avenue, one of Washington's grand shopping streets. The new additions present one face to Prospect Street, a street of smaller scale with a mix of commercial and residential uses, and another to an alley opening onto Prospect Street. The resulting project has three different façades, ranging from four to five stories, addressing three different situations.

Second- and third-floor offices, over first-floor retail space, will become the new home of the building's developer. Above that are five new residential apartments, no two alike, with some in the historic buildings and some in the new spaces.

Façade materials vary as one moves around the site and through the block, acknowledging and extending the rhythm of the original four buildings and the neighborhood.

The project is not seen as a single building but instead as a piece of the city, or even as a tiny city of its own, with living, working, and shopping all in one place.

Top right Model
Bottom right Building section
Opposite top Street façade
Opposite bottom left Entry
Opposite bottom right Aerial view showing alley façades

St. Michaels Community Center

St. Michaels, Maryland
Design 2022

The mission of St. Michaels Community Center is to promote the well-being of the community by providing quality affordable recreational, social, and educational activities to residents of all ages.

The current building housing the SMCC— a 1940s, largely unchanged, former lumberyard warehouse shed—was in serious disrepair and desperately in need of upgrades to meet current requirements.

Working within a vernacular aesthetic, a new plan has been woven through the post and beam structure. A new second-floor mezzanine houses the offices, freeing up space for program use on the first floor. Clerestory windows following the roof ridge bring much-needed light deeply into the central spaces.

The entry is opened up, allowing the interior vitality to now be visible from the street, contributing to the active fabric of St. Michaels. A strong new physical presence for the center will now match its already existing strong social presence in the town.

Top right Site and vicinity plan
Bottom right Current street view with original building before renovation
Opposite top Central space with offices above
Opposite bottom left New street façade
Opposite bottom right View from street

Firm Profiles

McInturff Architects

McInturff Architects is a five-person studio dedicated to the making of modern, highly crafted residential, commercial, and small institutional projects. The firm size is intentionally kept small to allow for close interaction within the studio and with clients and builders.

While all the work of the studio can be characterized as modern, there is no single style associated with the projects. Instead, the aesthetic of each is tailored to its specific program, location, and client.

The work of the firm has received more than 400 design awards, and has been frequently published, locally, nationally, and internationally. Three previous monographs, *In Detail: McInturff Architects* (2001), *In Residence: McInturff Architects* (2007), and *In House: McInturff Architects* (2013), were all published by the Images Publishing Group.

Mark McInturff, FAIA

Mark McInturff was a member of the first graduating class of the School of Architecture at the University of Maryland. After working three years as a carpenter to learn construction, he joined the firm of highly regarded Washington architect John Wiebenson, known for his activism and passion for socially responsible design. In 1986, McInturff founded McInturff Architects, focusing on small and medium-sized carefully crafted projects.

McInturff has taught at both the University of Maryland and the Catholic University of America. In addition to his role as studio critic, he led more than twenty student trips in the United States, Europe, and Asia, where he could share his passion for architecture with the upcoming generations of young architects.

McInturff was elevated to the College of Fellows of the AIA in 2000.

Project Credits

All plans, renderings, diagrams, and illustrations are supplied courtesy McInturff Architects. Photography is specified, as indicated.

21st Century Cabin (156–61)
Highland, Maryland (2016)
Design team: Mark McInturff, FAIA
General contractor: Timber Ridge Builders
Photography: Julia Heine
Awards: 2020 Residential Design Architecture Award; 2016 AIA DC/Washingtonian Residential Award; 2016 AIA Maryland Honor Award; 2016 AIA Potomac Valley Merit Award

43rd Street Townhouse (196–97)
Washington, DC (2017)
Design team: Mark McInturff, FAIA; Jeffrey McInturff
Owner/client: Yvonne Craver
General contractor: Acadia Contractors
Photography: Julia Heine

ADU Crestwood (132–35)
Washington, DC (2021)
Design team: Mark McInturff, FAIA; David Mogensen, AIA
General contractor: Acadia Contractors
Landscape architect: Lila Fendrick Landscape Architects
Lighting: Hinson Design Group, LLC.
Photography: Anice Hoachlander

Art Works Now (242–45)
Hyattsville, Maryland (2017)
Design team: Mark McInturff, FAIA; Colleen Healey, AIA
Owner/client: White Angelica, LLC.
General contractor: Added Dimensions, Inc.
Photography: Julia Heine
Awards: 2021 AIA Potomac Valley Citation; 2020 AIA Maryland Citation

Chain Bridge House (10–19)
Arlington, Virginia (2018)
Design team: Mark McInturff, FAIA; Colleen Healey, AIA; Peter Noonan, AIA
General contractor: Added Dimensions, Inc.
Photography: Colleen Healey (11); Julia Heine (12–18, 19 top); Angie Seckinger (19 bottom)
Awards: 2021 AIA Maryland Merit Award; 2018 AIA Potomac Valley Merit Award

Chesapeake Bay House (66–73)
Neavitt, Maryland (2011)
Design team: Mark McInturff, FAIA; Christopher Boyd, AIA
Owner/client: Mark McInturff
General contractor: McInturff Architects
Landscape design: Jan Kirsh Landscapes, Ltd.
Photography: Julia Heine (67–71, 72 bottom, 73), Mark McInturff (72 top)
Awards: 2015 AIA Potomac Valley Honor Award; 2013 AIA DC/Washingtonian Residential Award: 2012 AIA Maryland Citation; 2012 AIA Chesapeake Bay Honor Award

Del Ray House (106–7)
Bethesda, Maryland (2023)
Design team: Mark McInturff, FAIA; David Mogensen, AIA
Owner/client: Donna Afshar & Reza Farshey
General contractor: Added Dimensions, Inc.
Lighting design: Hinson Design Group, LLC.

Edmund Street House (184–87)
Washington, DC (2017)
Design team: Mark McInturff, FAIA; Colleen Healey, AIA; David Mogensen, AIA
General contractor: Added Dimensions, Inc.
Photography: Julia Heine (186, 187 top); Mark McInturff (185, 187 bottom)

Georgetown House (162–69)
Washington, DC (2018)
Design team: Phase 1 Mark McInturff, FAIA; Julia Heine; Phase 3 Mark McInturff, FAIA; Colleen Healey, AIA
General contractor: Phase 1 Acadia Contractors; Phase 3 Taylor Concepts
Interior design: MRJ Design Group
Photography: Anice Hoachlander (163, 164–65, 167, 168 top); Julia Heine (166, 168 bottom, 169)
Awards: 2022 Residential Design Citation; 2020 AIA DC/Washingtonian Residential Award; 2019 AIA Maryland Merit Award

Georgetown Mixed-Use (246–47)
Washington, DC (2022)
Design team: Mark McInturff, FAIA; Peter Noonan, AIA; David Mogensen, AIA
Owner/client: EastBanc Inc.
General contractor: Davis Construction
Lighting design: CM Kling + Associates

Georgian Modern (120–25)
Washington, DC (2020)
Design team: Mark McInturff, FAIA; Colleen Healey, AIA
General contractor: JWL Woodworking
Landscape architect: Lila Fendrick Landscape Architects
Interior design: Hendrick Interiors
Photography: Anice Hoachlander
Awards: 2021 AIA Maryland Design Award; 2021 Residential Design Architecture Award

Greencourt Innovation Center (202–11)
Rockville, Maryland (2017)
Design team: Mark McInturff, FAIA; Peter Noonan, AIA; David Mogensen, AIA
Owner/client: Greencourt Group, LLC.
General contractor: Meridian Construction Company, Inc.
Landscape architect: Stantec Consulting Services, Inc.
Lighting design: Hartranft Lighting Design
Photography: Julia Heine (203, 204, 205 bottom, 206–11); Anice Hoachlander (200, 205 top)
Awards: 2018 AIA DC Award of Excellence in Adaptive Reuse; 2018 AIA Maryland Honor Award; 2017 AIA Potomac Valley Honor Award; 2017 Montgomery County Design Excellence Award

A House in a Clearing (20–29)
Owings Mill, Maryland (2022)
Design team: Mark McInturff, FAIA; Jeffrey McInturff
Owner/client: Adam & Liz Gerber
General contractor: Design Alternatives, Inc.
Photography: Julia Heine (21–24, 25 top, 26–29); Jeffrey McInturff (25 bottom left); Mark McInturff (25 bottom right)

House in Kenwood (188–91)
Bethesda, Maryland (2016)
Design team: Mark McInturff, FAIA; Colleen Healey, AIA
Owner/client: Richard Creighton & Jane Ottenberg
General contractor: Alliance Builders, LLC.
Photography: Anice Hoachlander
Awards: 2019 AIA Maryland Merit Award; 2018 AIA Potomac Valley Gold Award for Best Residential Design; 2018 AIA Potomac Valley Merit Award; 2016 AIA DC/Washingtonian Residential Award

House on Deep Creek Lake (104–5)
Swanton, Maryland (2023)
Design team: Mark McInturff, FAIA; Julia Jeffs; Peter Noonan, AIA
Owner/client: Douglas & Sheriece Matias Dick
General contractor: Gosnell Builders

House on Indian River Bay (50–57)
Bethany Beach, Delaware (2019)
Design team: Mark McInturff, FAIA; Peter Noonan, AIA
Owner/client: Donna & Harold Gray
General contractor: Hugh H. Hickman & Sons, Inc.
Landscape architect: DCA Landscape Architects, Inc.
Photography: Julia Heine (51, 52 top, 53–57); Mark McInturff (52 bottom right); Radenko Ivanovic / 3D Photo Media (52 bottom left)

House on Maxmore Creek (150–55)
Royal Oak, Maryland (2018)
Design team: Mark McInturff, FAIA; Christopher Boyd, AIA; Jeffrey McInturff
Owner/client: Mary Beth Durkin & Hugh Panero
General contractor: ThinkMakeBuild
Primary photography: Julia Heine (151–52, 154–55); Mark McInturff (153)
Awards: 2018 AIA Chesapeake Bay Citation

House on Poplar Avenue (192–95)
Takoma Park, Maryland (2013)
Design team: Mark McInturff, FAIA; Colleen Healey, AIA
Owner/client: Alan Kanner
General contractor: Added Dimensions, Inc.
Photography: Julia Heine
Awards: 2016 AIA DC/*Washingtonian* Residential Award; 2015 AIA Maryland Merit Award; 2015 AIA Potomac Valley Merit Award; 2013 Metal Construction Association Chairman's Award; 2013 *Remodeling* Merit Award

House on Tilghman Creek (96–103)
Claiborne, Maryland (2017)
Design team: Mark McInturff, FAIA; Christopher Boyd, AIA; Jeffrey McInturff
Owner/client: Martin & Maura Bollinger
General contractor: ThinkMakeBuild
Landscape design: McHale Landscape Design
Photography: Julia Heine (97–98, 99 bottom, 101–3); Jeffrey McInturff (99 top); Mark McInturff (100)
Awards: 2021 AIA Chesapeake Merit Award; 2018 *Annapolis Home* Builder & Fine Design Grand Award

House. Pool. Garden. (40–49)
Washington, DC (2020)
Design team: Mark McInturff, FAIA; Colleen Healey, AIA
General contractor: Zantzinger, Inc.
Landscape architect: Lila Fendrick Landscape Architects
Exterior lighting design: Outdoor Illuminations
Photography: Anice Hoachlander (41–46, 47 bottom right, 48); Julia Heine (47 top right, 49)
Awards: 2020 AIA DC/*Washingtonian* Residential Award; 2020 AIA Maryland Merit Award; 2020 AIA Potomac Valley Gold Award for Best Residential Design

Hutner Porch & Pool (174–79)
Chevy Chase, Maryland (2016)
Design team: Mark McInturff, FAIA; Peter Noonan, AIA
Owner/client: David & Susan Hutner
General contractor: Timber Ridge Builders
Landscape design: Carolyn Mullet
Photography: Julia Heine
Awards: 2018 AIA DC Merit Award in Architecture; 2018 AIA DC/*Washingtonian* Residential Award; 2017 AIA Potomac Valley Citation; 2016 AIA Maryland Merit Award; 2016 *Remodeling* Design Award

Library House (30–39)
Potomac, Maryland (2021)
Design team: *Phase 1* Mark McInturff, FAIA; Peter Noonan, AIA; *Phase 2* Mark McInturff, FAIA; David Mogensen, AIA; Peter Noonan, AIA
General contractor: *Phase 1* West Wing Builders; *Phase 2* Added Dimensions, Inc.
Photography: Anice Hoachlander (31–33, 35, 36–37, 39); Julia Heine (34, 38)
Awards: 2022 AIA DC/*Washingtonian* Residential Award; 2021 AIA Maryland Merit Award

Live/Work (112–19)
Montgomery County, Maryland (2019)
Design team: Mark McInturff, FAIA; Peter Noonan, AIA
General contractor: Alliance Builders, Inc.
Landscape architect: Gregg Bleam Landscape Architects
Lighting design: Hartranft Lighting Design
Photography: Anice Hoachlander

López Forastier-Hellmann House (180–83)
Chevy Chase, Maryland (2018)
Design team: Mark McInturff, FAIA; Jeffrey McInturff
Owner/client: Peta Hellmann & Miguel López Forastier
General contractor: Lofgren Construction
Photography: Anice Hoachlander

McDaniel Marsh House (58–65)
Rehoboth Beach, Delaware (2016)
Design team: Mark McInturff, FAIA
Owner/client: Patricia McDaniel
General contractor: Boardwalk Builders
Photography: Julia Heine
Awards: 2017 AIA Potomac Valley Merit Award

Multigenerational House in Jamaica (108–9)
Jamaica (Design 2022)
Design team: Mark McInturff, FAIA; Julia Jeffs
Owner/client: Heather & Kevin Reid

Parker Metal (212–17)
Baltimore, Maryland (2018)
Design team: Mark McInturff, FAIA; David Mogensen, AIA; Christopher Boyd, AIA
Owner/client: Himmelrich Associates, Inc.
General contractor: Inland Builders, LLC.
Interior design: Rory McCarthy Design
Lighting design: Bliss-Fasman
Photography: Julia Heine (214 top, 215–17); Patrick Ross (213, 214 bottom)
Awards: 2019 AIA DC Award for Excellence in Architecture; 2019 AIA Maryland Honor Award; 2019 AIA Potomac Valley Honor Award; 2019 AIA Baltimore Excellence in Design Award; 2019 AIA Baltimore Trostel Award for Excellence in Historic Preservation; 2019 AIA Chesapeake Bay Honor Award

Politics and Prose (236–41)
Washington, DC (2018)
Design team: Mark McInturff, FAIA; Colleen Healey, AIA
Owner/client: Bradley Graham & Lissa Muscatine
General contractor: Added Dimensions, Inc.
Photography: Julia Heine
Awards: 2019 AIA DC Award for For Excellence in Interior Architecture; 2019 AIA Maryland Merit Award; 2018 AIA Potomac Valley Citation

Porter Street House (146–49)
Washington, DC (2015)
Design team: Mark McInturff, FAIA; Jeffrey McInturff
Owner/client: Meghan Draheim & David Harris
General contractor: Added Dimensions, Inc.
Photography: Julia Heine

Ranleigh Road Library (170–73)
Arlington, Virginia (2018)
Design team: Mark McInturff, FAIA; Peter Noonan, AIA
Owner/client: Victoria Nuland & Robert Kagan
General contractor: Acadia Contractors
Photography: Julia Heine

Rappahannock Bend Summer House (88–91)
King George, Virginia (2009)
Design team: Mark McInturff, FAIA; Colleen Healey, AIA
General contractor: Bonitt Builders
Landscape architect: Crowther Landscape Architects
Photography: Julia Heine
Awards: 2013 AIA DC Chapter Design Award; 2011 AIA DC/Washingtonian Residential Award; 2010 Custom Home Merit Award; 2010 AIA Maryland Honor Award; 2010 Builder's Choice Award; 2009 AIA Potomac Valley Grand Honor Award

Reid Beach House (74–79)
Bethany Beach, Delaware (2019)
Design team: Mark McInturff, FAIA; Christopher Boyd, AIA; Jeffrey McInturff; Julia Jeffs; David Mogensen, AIA
Owner/client: Heather & Kevin Reid
General contractor: Timothy B. O'Hare Custom Builder, Inc.
Landscape design: Mike O'Hare
Interior design: Transitions by Sharon Kleinman
Photography: Julia Heine

Ridge House (92–95)
Little Washington, Virginia (2013)
Design team: Mark McInturff, FAIA; David Mogensen AIA
Owner/client: Kevin Adams & Jay Brown
General contractor: Opitz Construction
Photography: Julia Heine
Awards: 2015 AIA Maryland Merit Award; 2015 AIA Potomac Valley Merit Award

Singh Hoysted Live/Work (80–87)
Bethesda, Maryland (2015)
Design team: Mark McInturff, FAIA; Colleen Healey, AIA
Owner/client: Jackie Hoysted & Prem Singh
General contractor: Added Dimensions, Inc.
Photography: Julia Heine
Awards: 2016 AIA DC/*Washingtonian* Residential Award; 2016 AIA Potomac Valley Merit Award; 2015 AIA Maryland Honor Award

St. Michaels Community Center (248–49)
St. Michaels, Maryland (Design 2022)
Design team: Mark McInturff, FAIA; Christopher Boyd, AIA; Jeffrey McInturff; Julia Jeffs
Owner/client: St Michaels Community Center

Truss House (136–39)
Bethesda, Maryland (2021)
Design team: Mark McInturff, FAIA;
Owner/client: Lisa Comer & Chris Cosby
General contractor: Timber Ridge Builders
Photography: Julia Heine

Urban Courtyard Apartments (218–23)
Washington, DC (2018)
Design team: Mark McInturff, FAIA; Peter Noonan, AIA
Owner/client: Ditto Residential
General contractor: Harbor Builders
Landscape architect: Lila Fendrick Landscape Architects
Custom stair: Hiroshi Jacobs
Photography: Julia Heine (219–20, 221 left, 222–23); Mark McInturff (221 right)
Awards: 2019 AIA DC Award for Excellence in Architecture; 2019 AIA DC/Washingtonian Residential Award; 2019 AIA Maryland Honor Award; 2019 AIA Potomac Valley Citation

Watergate East Lobbies (224–31)
Washington, DC (2019)
Design team: Mark McInturff, FAIA; Julia Heine, David Mogensen, AIA; Jeffrey McInturff
Owner/client: Watergate East
General contractor: Added Dimensions, Inc.
Lighting design: Flux Studio, Ltd.
Interior design: Julia Heine
Photography: Anice Hoachlander
Awards: 2019 AIA Maryland Honor Award

Woodley Park House & Garden (140–45)
Washington, DC (2018)
Design team: Mark McInturff, FAIA; Colleen Healey, AIA
General contractor: Lofgren Construction
Landscape architect: Lila Fendrick Landscape Architects
Photography: Julia Heine
Awards: 2018 AIA Maryland Merit Award

Woodmont 17th Floor (126–31)
Bethesda, Maryland (2021)
Design team: Mark McInturff, FAIA; David Mogensen, AIA
General contractor: Added Dimensions, Inc.
Lighting design: Hinson Design Group, LLC.
Interior design: Sophie Prévost/ColePrévost; Susan A. Vallon, Ltd.
Photography: Anice Hoachlander

The Writer's Center (232–35)
Bethesda, Maryland (*Phase 1* 2014; *Phase 2* 2019)
Design team: *Phase 1* Mark McInturff, FAIA; Julia Heine, Jeffrey McInturff; *Phase 2* Mark McInturff, FAIA; Colleen Healey, AIA
Owner/client: The Writer's Center
General contractor: Added Dimensions, Inc.
Photography: Julia Heine
Awards: 2021 Montgomery County Design Excellence Citation; 2020 AIA Maryland Citation; 2020 AIA Potomac Valley Merit Award

Xia Yang House (198–99)
McLean, Virginia (2023)
Design team: Mark McInturff, FAIA; Jeffrey McInturff
Owner/client: Tain Xia & Kacy Yang
General contractor: Acadia Contractors

Selected Published Works

2022

"2022 RD Architecture Awards," *Residential Design*, 2022, vol. 3, pp. 86–89, 97.

Conroy, S. Claire, "Worth the Wait: Library for 10,000 Books," *Residential Design*, 2022, vol.1, pp. 15–17.

Liebowitz, Denise, "Cabinet of Curiosities," *ArchitectureDC*, Spring 2022, pp. 50–55.

Taylor, Kymberly, "A Sea of White in Georgetown," *Annapolis Home Magazine*, 2022, vol. 13, no. 2, pp. 29–35.

2021

"2021 RD Architecture Awards," *Residential Design*, 2021, vol. 3, p. 94.

"AIA Honor Winners!" *Annapolis Home Magazine*, 2021, vol. 12, no. 3, p. 65.

Brown, Oliver C., "Buying Your Eastern Shore Home," *Senior Services Source Book 2020/2021*, pp. 38–39.

Hales, Linda, "Shaft of Light," *Home & Design*, November/December 2021, pp. 74–85.

Moeller, G. Martin, "Scribe Vibe: Writers Find Welcoming Environment in a Former Youth Center," *ArchitectureDC*, Winter 2021, pp. 70–71.

Weber, Cheryl, "2021 RDAA | Georgian Modern | McInturff Architects," *Residential Design*, 5 August 2021.

2020

"2020 RD Architecture Awards," *Residential Design*, 2020, vol. 3, pp. 62–63.

Dan, Sharon Jaffe, "Unfettered Spirit: Organic Elements and Natural Light Define a Zen Escape," *Home & Design*, July/August 2020.

Heubeck, Elizabeth, "Seaside Modern," *Annapolis Home Magazine*, 2020, vol. 11, no. 4.

Liebowitz, Denise, "Parallel Lines," *ArchitectureDC*, Spring 2020, pp. 34–39.

Moeller, G. Martin, "The Convertible House: Bayfront Residence Sits Lightly on the Land," *ArchitectureDC*, Winter 2020, pp. 56–60.

Moeller, G. Martin, "Metropolitan Homes: New Houses Across the Region Offer Varied Takes on Modern Living," *ArchitectureDC*, Fall 2020, p. 66.

Sanders, Julie, "Tower Vista," *Home & Design/Chesapeake Views*, Winter 2020.

Sanders, Julie, "Perfect Fit," *Home & Design*, September 2020, pp. 98–106.

Weber, Cheryl, "2020 RDAA | 21st Century Cabin | McInturff Architects," *Residential Design*, 20 July 2020.

2019

Dan, Sharon Jaffe, "Seaside Oasis," *Home & Design*, Summer 2019, pp. 266–73.

Duva, Louis, "Commercial Interests: Three Diverse Projects Offer New Models for the Workplace," *ArchitectureDC*, Fall 2019, pp. 24–27.

Kashino, Marisa M., "The Lake House," *Washingtonian*, February 2019, pp. 134–35.

Kashino, Marisa M., "Washington's Top 9 New Houses of the Year," *Washingtonian*, August 2019.

Martella, Jennifer, "Spy House of the Week: Modernism by a Master" *The Talbot Spy*, 2 April 2019.

O'Rourke, Ronald, "Strength in Numbers: Multi-family Projects Get their Due," *ArchitectureDC*, Fall 2019, pp. 52–53.

Weber, Cheryl, "Case Study: Chain Bridge House by McInturff Architects," *Residential Design*, 2019, vol. 4, pp. 68–76.

"The Winners: The Annapolis Home Builder and Fine Design Awards," *Annapolis Home Magazine*, 2019, vol. 10, no. 1, pp. 46–47.

Zemanski, Renee Houston, "Marshland Modernity," *Annapolis Home Magazine*, 2019, vol. 10, no. 3, pp. 32–42, cover.

2018

"Architecture of the Shore," *Shore Monthly*, March 2018, pp. 52–53.

Dickens, Steven K., "Innovative Office and Retail Projects," *ArchitectureDC*, Winter 2018, p. 40.

Dietsch, Deborah K., "Balancing Act," *Home & Design*, November/December 2018, pp. 100–107.

Kashino, Marisa M., "Hot Properties," *Washingtonian*, August 2018, pp. 69.

"Marshland Idyll," *Home & Design Sourcebook*, 2018, pp. 82–83.

O'Rourke, Ronald, "Little Gems: Small Residential Projects with Big Impact," *ArchitectureDC*, Winter 2018, pp. 76–77.

Thompson, Boyce, *Anatomy of a Great Home: What America's Most Celebrated Houses Tell Us about the Way We Want to Live* (Pennsylvania: Schiffer Publishing, 2018): pp. 100–103, 170, 182–85.

2017

Brillon, James, "McInturff Architects renovates home without furniture in Maryland," *Dezeen*, 2 January 2017.

Conroy, S. Claire, "A House of Her Own," *Residential Design*, 2017, vol. 1, pp. 46–49.

Dan, Sharon Jaffe, "High Tech Hub," *Home & Design*, September/October 2017, p. 248.

Dickens, Steven K., "Home Is Where the Innovation Is: A Residential Architect Branches into Commercial Design," *ArchitectureDC*, Fall 2017, pp. 42–47.

Edelson, Harriet, "The Trick to Transforming a House into a Magic Box," *The Washington Post Real Estate*, 19 January 2017, pp. 12–14, cover.

Goldchain, Michelle, "The D.C. Area's 8 Most Beautiful Homes of 2017," *Curbed DC*, 22 December 2017.

Kashino, Marisa M., "Haute Houses," *Washingtonian*, August 2017, p. 79.

Moeller, G. Martin, "Less is More Rewarding: Renovation Preserved Clients' Thoughtful Austerity," *ArchitectureDC*, Summer 2017, pp. 20–24.

Taylor, Kymberly, "A Modern Breeze Blows Through It," *Annapolis Home Magazine*, 2017, vol. 8, no. 4, pp. 28–35.

2016

O'Rourke, Ronald, "Un-Suburbia: Six Houses Offer New Ideas for 21st Century Lives," *ArchitectureDC*, Winter 2016, pp. 26–27, 32, 35–36.

2015

Dietsch, Deborah K., "Letting work and life mix in one perfect home," *The Washington Post*, 25 February 2015.

2014

Dan, Sharon Jaffe, "Back to Nature," *Home & Design*, January/February 2014, pp. 120–29.

Levine, Tom, "An Architectural Jewel Box," *Annapolis Home Magazine*, 2014, vol. 5, no. 4, pp. 31–39, cover.

2013

Dickens, Steven K., "Shore: Living on the Waterfront," *ArchitectureDC*, Summer 2013, pp. 48–49.

Dietsch, Deborah K., "Lofty Living," *Home & Design*, September/October 2013, pp. 106–15.

McInturff, Mark and Julia Heine, *In House: McInturff Architects* (Melbourne, Australia: Images Publishing, 2013).

Moeller, G. Martin, "Suburbs: Houses Amidst the Trees," *ArchitectureDC*, Summer 2013, pp. 30–31.

Orton, Kathy, "A Masterpiece of Artful Design," *The Washington Post*, 26 January 2013, p. E2.

2012

"A New Beginning," *Dwell*, October 2012, pp. 78–86.

Dietsch, Deborah K., "The Architect's Getaway," *The Washington Post*, 28 April 2012, pp. E1, E3.

Herman, Beth, "Circling the Wagons—21st Century Style," *DC Mud*, 28 January 2012.

Maynard, Nigel F., "Bay Watch: Bethesda architect Mark McInturff designs a weekend retreat with a modern, quirky sensibility," *Bethesda Magazine*, July/August 2012.

2011

Dietsch, Deborah K., "Modern Reinvention," *Home & Design*, Fall 2011, pp. 112–133, cover.

Eck, Jeremiah, *House in the Landscape: Siting Your House Naturally*, Princeton Architectural Press, 2011, pp. 180–187.

McInturff, Mark, "Tweaking Tradition," *Inform*, 2011, no. 2, pp. 10–13.

Parven, Cari Shane, "City Stickers: In Kalorama, an urban roost with room for all," *Washington Post Magazine*, 30 March 2011, pp. 28–35.

2010

Dansicker, Jennifer K., "Face to Face with Architect Mark McInturff," *Chesapeake Home + Living*, June 2010.

Herman, Beth, "The Architect Also Rises," *DC Mud*, 7 October 2010.

Liebowitz, Denise, "Oak Allee: New House Responds to Landscape in an Unexpected Way," *ArchitectureDC*, Summer 2010, pp. 20–21.

Maynard, Nigel F., Cheryl Weber, Meghan Drueding, and Bruce D. Snider, "ra50: The Short List of Architects We Love," *residential architect*, November/December 2010, p. 40.

McInturff, Mark, FAIA, "Coming back for More," *ArchitectureDC*, Summer 2010, pp. 40–43.

Moeller, G. Martin, Jr., "Living Lightly: Two Residential Projects Barely Touch the Ground," *ArchitectureDC*, Winter 2010, p. 26.

——, "Stairs That Soar," *ArchitectureDC*, Winter 2010, p. 26.

Parven, Cari Shane, "Spare & Serene," *Home & Design*, Spring 2010, pp. 104–13.

2009

"A Treehouse-Style Solution," *Washington Spaces*, Spring 2009, pp. 94–95.

"Great Gains but Little Added," *Washington Spaces*, Fall 2009, pp. 90–91.

Sapienza, Terri, "The Perfect House, Take 2," *The Washington Post*, 1 October 2009, pp. B01, B04.

2008

Groer, Annie, "Merging the New with the Old," *The Washington Post*, 12 June 2008, pp. 16–19.

Keates, Nancy, "Home Front: Design Within Reach," *The Wall Street Journal*, 21 November 2008.

2007

McInturff, Mark and Julia Heine, *In Residence: McInturff Architects* (Melbourne, Australia: Images Publishing, 2007).

Moeller, Sherry, "Posts & Beams," *Washington Spaces*, Spring 2007, pp. 129–35.

Stanley, Kathleen, "Back to the City," *Custom Home*, Winter 2007, pp. 114–17.

2006

Barbour, David, "A New Home for New Plays," *Lighting & Sound America*, February 2006, pp. 56–61.

Dietsch, Deborah K., "Modern Counterpoint," *Home & Design*, November/December 2006.

Drueding, Meghan, "The Educations of Mark McInturff," *Custom Home*, Fall 2006, pp. 68–79.

Gerchak, Keith, "Planning the Regional Theater," *Lighting & Sound America*, June 2006.

Gunts, Edward, "Seaside Loft," *Waterfront Home & Design*, Spring 2006, pp. 72–81.

Groer, Annie, "Modern Love," *Washington Post Magazine*, 23 April 2006, p. H01.

Hyatt, Peter, *Out of Town: The Country House* (Melbourne, Australia: Images Publishing, 2006) pp. 212–15.

Karth, Barbara, "Pure Geometry," *Home & Design*, March/April 2006, pp. 138–49, 214.

Knowles, Ralph L., *Ritual House: Drawing on Nature's Rhythms for Architecture and Urban Design* (Island Press 2006), cover.

Maynard, Nigel F., Meghan Drueding, and Shelley D. Hutchins, "Leftover Overhauls," *residential architect*, August 2006, pp. 52–56.

Trulove, James Grayson, *25 Apartments and Lofts Under 2500 Square Feet* (Harper Design/HarperCollins, 2006), pp. 84–91.

2005

Beaver, Robyn (ed.), *100 More of the World's Best Houses* (Melbourne, Australia: Images Publishing, 2005), pp. 110–13.

Gorlin, Alexander, *Creating the New American Townhouse* (New York: Rizzoli International, 2005).

Hasanovic, Aisha (ed.), *50 Great Kitchens by Architects* (Melbourne, Australia: Images Publishing, 2005), pp. 6–7.

2004

Connell, John, *Creating the Inspired House* (Connecticut: Taunton Press, 2004), pp. 98–107.

Details in Architecture: Volume 5 (Melbourne, Australia: Images Publishing, 2004), pp. 172–75.

Karth, Barbara, "Playing with Light," *Home & Design*, Spring 2004, pp. 140–53.

——, "Ocean View," *Waterfront Home & Design*, Spring 2004, pp. 26–33.

Lawson, Todd and Connor, Tom, The House to Ourselves (Connecticut: Taunton Press, 2004), pp. 58–67.

Snider, Bruce D., "Custom Home of the Year," *Custom Home*, September/October 2004, pp. 94–99.

Trulove, James Grayson, *New American Interiors* (Whitney Library of Design/Watson-Guptill, 2004), pp. 170–77.

——, *Tree Houses by Architects* (Harper Design International/HarperCollins, 2004), pp. 42–51.

——, *Living Outside Inside* (Harper Design International/HarperCollins, 2004), pp. 70–79, 114–23.

——, *Cottages: The New Style* (Harper Design International/HarperCollins, 2004), pp.42–49, 70–77, 114–21.

2003

Boschetti, Joe (ed.), *Social Spaces: Volume 2* (Melbourne, Australia: Images Publishing, 2003), pp. 164–67.

Eck, Jeremiah, *The Distinctive Home: A Vision of Timeless Design* (Connecticut: Taunton Press/American Institute of Architects 2003).

McCausland, Christianna, "The Mark of Good Design," *Baltimore Magazine*, October 2003, pp. 145–49.

2002

Clagett, Leslie Plummer, *The New City Home* (Connecticut: Taunton Press, 2002): pp. 202–9.

Davis, Jodie and Strong, Diane (eds.), *100 of the World's Best Houses* (Melbourne, Australia: Images Publishing, 2002), pp. 92–95.

Details in Architecture: Volume 4 (Melbourne, Australia: Images Publishing, 2002), pp. 122–37.

Powers, Kelly, "Let There Be Light," *Baltimore Magazine*, October 2002, pp. 124–27.

2001

Details in Architecture: Volume 3 (Melbourne, Australia: Images Publishing, 2001) pp. 116–23.

McInturff, Mark and Julia Heine, *In Detail: McInturff Architects* (Melbourne, Australia: Images Publishing, 2001).

Published in Australia in 2022 by
The Images Publishing Group Pty Ltd
ABN 89 059 734 431

Offices

Melbourne
Waterman Business Centre
Suite 64, Level 2 UL40
1341 Dandenong Road
Chadstone, Victoria 3148
Australia
Tel: +61 3 8564 8122

New York
6 West 18th Street 4B
New York City, NY 10011
United States
Tel: +1 212 645 1111

Shanghai
6F, Building C, 838 Guangji Road
Hongkou District, Shanghai 200434
China
Tel: +86 021 31260822

books@imagespublishing.com
www.imagespublishing.com

Copyright © McInturff Architects 2022
The Images Publishing Group Reference Number: 1533

All photography is attributed in the Project Credits on pages 251–53 unless otherwise noted.
Page 4: Anice Hoachlander (House. Pool. Garden.; Washington, DC); page 8: Anice Hoachlander (Library House; Potomac, Maryland); page 110: Anice Hoachlander (Georgian Modern; Washington, DC); page 200: Anice Hoachlander (Greencourt Innovation Center; Rockville, Maryland)

All rights reserved. Apart from any fair dealing for the purposes of private study, research, criticism or review as permitted under the Copyright Act, no part of this publication may be reproduced, stored in a retrieval system, or transmitted in any form by any means, electronic, mechanical, photocopying, recording or otherwise, without the written permission of the publisher.

 A catalogue record for this book is available from the National Library of Australia

Title: HomeWork: New Houses | Changed Houses | Not Houses // McInturff Architects
ISBN: 9781864708592

This title was commissioned in IMAGES' Melbourne office and produced as follows:
Editorial Georgia (Gina) Tsarouhas, *Graphic design* Ryan Marshall, *Production* Nicole Boehringer

Printed on 157gsm Chinese OJI matt art paper (FSC®) by Artron Art (Group) Co., Ltd, in China

IMAGES has included on its website a page for special notices in relation to this and its other publications.
Please visit www.imagespublishing.com

Every effort has been made to trace the original source of copyright material contained in this book.
The publishers would be pleased to hear from copyright holders to rectify any errors or omissions.

The information and illustrations in this publication have been prepared and supplied by McInturff Architects.
While all reasonable efforts have been made to ensure accuracy, the publishers do not, under any circumstances, accept responsibility for errors, omissions and representations express or implied.